LEADERSHIP

BEING A LEADER
Historically and Today

LEADERSHIP

Being a Leader
Historically and Today

ASIN: B09B35B36G

Jacked Design & Illustrations © Guebres Studios

ISBN-13: 979532369337 (sc)

Printed in the United States of America
CreateSpace date: 07/24/2021

PREFACE

I had thought to do as I usual do, and bury the lede. Since this topic of leaders and leadership is proving important, thhat's exactly what I will continue do.

Many do not want to be leaders, even though they have the right instincts to take a commanding role.

Many want to be leaders, even though they are totally unsuited for the position.

But, for the average person – the complacent herd member – the real issue is being able to recognize who are the con-artists and who are the true leaders.

And, with that assertion, you get your first hint: The con-artist will always attack, but never offer an alternative solution or put forth a viable alternative approach. All too often, the con-artist will call upon you to place your ego above the evidence of your eyes and experience. For those who need examples, that's was the basis for Hans Christian Andersen's story, "The Emperor's New Clothes," first published on 7 April 1837.

That was the same year Karl Marx wrote a letter to his father which opened with the words: *"There are life-moments that, like border markers, stand before an expiring time while at the same time clearly pointing out a new direction."*

Marx was communicating personally to his father – he was a 19-year-old scholar emerging into a changing world. It was the year of the Daguerreotype; in two years, the word photography would be coined; three years earlier, The Slavery Abolition Act had gone into effect throughout the British Empire in 1834.

Some people saw the changes, others still marveled at the non-existent clothes. Think Trump Era: Border Wall, Smart phones, Twitter, Tic Tok, Covid-19 Stimulus, Progressives.

The names which survive are "true leaders" who recognized the reality around them.

This book is dedicated to the thousands of years of history and warnings, and a recognition that we are, again, experiencing a time of major transition.

CHAPTERS

CHAPTER One - Who is a Leader

Anyone can be a leader. For the wise, the defining issue is the order of magnitude – the level to which they aspire and to which they are best suited.

Each of us can identify a cliche example – the leader of the "in crowd" or "popular kids" in both grade school and then high school and then whatever incarnation we see in College or University. But are they really "Leaders"? Is that the role they will assume in "real life"?

TV sitcoms present us with the leader of the PTA, as the defining organizational driving force among the parents – a dominant force in a narrowly defined area of "civic activity." A parallel can be found in the character of the mother in the TV series "Young Sheldon" – one who organizes Church events and serves as a form of "moral police" seeking to exert control over others. In the real world, they gave us the Salem Witch Trials, Prohibition, and, when those failed, the laws against marijuana.

They are also *"Pro-Life"* – a position taken to provide more people for them to torture and kill. Their time as leaders passed with the Inquisition. It's a reality they have yet to fully acknowledge.

Obviously, we can look to the political – the city council, mayor, governor, local/state/federal representative, or Senator. And while politics has proved to be a career position for many, there are other career governmental positions – Chief of Police, head of the Sanitation Department – which are also leadership roles.

In the private sector, there are the business owners and managers – along with the consultants who advise them or are called upon to handle specific tasks such as those in the legal or accounting areas.

To be a leader who then assumes the true responsibilities of leadership is quite different from an individual who simply raises through the ranks and is granted responsibility by those who are true leaders.

That is, for many, a culturally disturbing idea – the idea that an apparent leader is not the leader, but only serves as the visible agent for true leaders. At the same time, we have no difficulty with the concept – a Commander-in-Chief gives the order, the Generals interpret that order, and that interpretation is then reinterpreted by the Field Command.

Leadership includes the delegation of responsibility but keeping the blame while sharing the credit.

On a broad societal level, we express both the idea, and our discomfort with it, in terms of "Secrete Cabals" or "Elites" who are, like the Wizard of Oz, functioning and controlling things from behind a curtain.

Part of that control is to target your audience. If you wish to address those who are true leaders, you need only drop a few terms that will scare off everyone who is not part of your target demographic. One of my personal favorites is to mention or make reference to the "BIBLE" – which is a document that was designed to simultaneously control "illiterate masses" while imparting wisdom to the "elite."

We are trained to view the Bible – or all scriptures from any religious belief system – in a sectarian and parochial way. If we go back to the dawn of writing, when things were pictorial, we are presented with people, Gods, and Demons. But when it came time to create the Hebrew Bible things changed – the old was accepted as the basis for attracting the masses, and the new was encoded for the wise.

By "new" I am referencing the "hidden wisdom" or what we would now term to be hard science. Those who are true leaders understand the concept or approach. They understand there are at least four human categories: the superstitious fool, the denier, the follower, and the leader.

The "superstitious" believe in magic or alien conspiracy

theories – as we shall see, they ignore fact-based logic. Their defining trait is an inability to believe or accept basic human intelligence as a basic contributor to our cultural development. Therefore there must be an interventionist deity and demons intervening to disrupt the "Devine Plan."

But, as will be demonstrated, their premise serves as the basis to challenge their beliefs. Moreover, their premise allows us to view "*evil*" as part of "*the divine plan*" through which they self-identify as being unworthy to obtain the desired "salvation" they claim to seek. They are not worthy of holding a leadership role. If they were, a Grand Inquisitor would rule the world.

This group believes that their all-knowing and perfect deity is so egotistical that it created humanity to worship it for all eternity and the driving force for every individual should be to earn the right to spend eternity in that worship.

Of course, based on the observed efficiency that defines the physical universe, were their deity all-powerful, it could have simply created the cheering section and programmed it to believe they were acting out of choice and exhibiting the free will to engage in the persistent declaring of praise and worship.

The superstitious do not grasp the logical problem and so are easily controlled and manipulated.

Granted, there was a time in the past where reliance on magical forces was logical. Such forces or entities served to explain that which is now explained through statistical analysis and science. Both of these are basic pattern recognition – when the pattern could not be discerned, "Lady Luck" and the various demons or angels served as a convenient scapegoat.

The superstitious tend to blame others for the fruits of their behavior. It is a practice that is also observed in acts of the denier.

Leaders look for patterns and reasons which they can then utilize, control, or reproduce - or allow for – whenever the need arises in their decision-making process. Understanding that patterns are a natural part of existence, a leader might seek to modify them. But they will not try to disrupt it – patterns are there to be used.

Rather than seek to reveal or explain observed patterns, the superstitious blame them on agents of some benevolent or malevolent entity or deity. Deniers simply deny their existence – the patterns become the *"elephant in the room."*

When invoking Supernatural Creatures like "Lady Luck," Sprites, Fairies, Leprechauns, other such folklore entities, the common element is capriciousness or some disruption of their natural environment.

Our second group, the deniers or naysayers, tend to be dismissive in a way that offers no rational alternative to that which they are rejecting and are generally indiscriminate and therefore often hypocritical. They attack something because the other side suggested it, or simply because they enjoy saying everyone else is wrong – while never offering an example of what would be correct.

A characteristic of this group is the denial of any facts which fail to conform to their preconceived belief system – as you might have immediately grasped, this is a trait which is also common among the superstitious. It is the next evolutionary step and comes into existence with the acceptance of facts over fantasy.

At this stage, when the individuals encounter evidence that should cause them to doubt their beliefs, they often react by rejecting the evidence and then strengthen their support for their original position. There are several terms for this reaction, one is Cognitive Dissidence, another is the "Backfire Effect."

During the late 19th century and well into the mid-20th century, the phrase "Banned in Boston" was used to describe a literary work, song, motion picture, or play considered to be too immoral or risque for the general public and so distribution or exhibition was prohibited in Boston, Massachusetts.

Prohibition was a national expansion of the puritanical religious nonsense behind that "Banned in Boston" mystique. At first, the loss of the Boston market was seen as a deterrent to various genres, but leaders soon realized that the Backfire Effect served to expand sales. They made use of it.

In many ways, obtaining rights to claiming something you were promoting was "Banned in Boston" became the goal. Prohibition served to expand the sale of alcoholic beverages and gave rise to the "speakeasy" culture and bootlegging – both of which served to define the Roaring Twenties.

Prohibition also served to establish "crime bosses" and "organized crime." The classic regional "outlaw gang" gave rise to the national Mafia or mob level that would dominate major population centers.

Leaders tend to take advantage of negatives. They like a Backfire Effect – it can create followers. Main Stream Media {MSM} attacks on Trump create a feedback loop that benefits both. And Trump understands and utilizes it.

Trump also employs the classic example of the concept "Lead by Following," which is embodied in a phrase generally attributed to a Napoleonic era politician – Alexandre Auguste Ledru-Rollin – *"There go the people. I must follow them, for I am their leader."*

A variation of this quote is attributed to the Marquis de Lafayette, who was supposedly having wine with a friend at a Paris bistro when the mob passed on the way to Storming the Bastille. It is said Lafayette suddenly gulped his wine and ran toward the mob.

His friend shouted, *"Where are you going?"*

To which Lafayette shouted back, *"With them!"*

The friend then yelled, *"Where are they going?"*

"I don't know!" was the reply.

Which elicited, *"Then why are you going?"*

To which Lafayette replied, "*Because I am their leader!*"

A leader is often someone who follows from the front and is unaware of where he is going. The initial stage is to assume the mantle of responsibility and be acknowledged in that role.

A leader is a stallion racing to the head of the stampeding herd; once there, the herd sees him, because of his physical position at the very front of the herd, as their leader. Once that recognition is made, wherever the stallion goes, the herd will follow. And it is only when the herd is willing to follow that the direction has meaning.

Many leaders hold that role because of the position and without any connection to the driving force or possible goal of those who follow them. For the herd, the only real goal is to fit in and be part of the herd. A herd is composed of followers.

If we were looking at a flock of geese during their annual migration, we would see a triangular formation whose leader is the bird that might be the strongest. As they fly, there seems to be a drafting effect that pulls the other birds and assists the weakest flyers – thus, the birds at the rear often are the weakest. They are also the wisest target for a hunter – if hit, the bird to the rear falls and other birds are unaware of the danger.

The flock is, in this way, dystopian – it is unaware of the reality and denies the meaning of the gunshot. It is only those who witness the fall of their companions who are aware of the true danger. Those who wish to lead will not expose themselves as they remove their competition or any obstacles in their path.

There is a natural cognitive bias that causes people who encounter evidence challenging their beliefs toward rejection. Since they are not directly affected, they will strengthen their support of their original stance and deny reality. We see this with Climate Change and anything else that requires years or decades to fully manifest itself.

It's the idea of placing a frog in a pot of cold water on a stove and then, turn on the stove and let the water gradually heat until it boils – and kills the frog.

The idea being that a gradual change can be accepted and adjusted until that point where it is too late to respond.

We play this same game with unfounded accusations in the context of a supposed moral position.

In the past, someone with a grasp on medical hygiene or the use of natural herbs might have been accused of witchcraft because they did not become ill and were able to cure those who did become ill.

The superstitious needed evidence to support beliefs so ignored the facts. As we shall see with the story of *The Flood*, leaders accept the belief and then alter the facts inherent in the belief to create a new belief system.

In recent years, superstition has given was to political correctness, and those who would assert an absolute acceptance of unsubstantiated decades-old sexual impropriety allegations on the part of a political nominee from another political party will ignore similar sworn allegations of misconduct by those in their own party. Selective denial and hypocrisy are behaviors loved by those who wish to manipulate society.

The approach to Justice Brett Kavanaugh and Andrew Cuomo serve as a model. Comically, when Kavanaugh denied the allegations, in September 2018, Cuomo called for him to take a lie-detector test. The issue was a 1982 high school party attended by Brett and his accuser, Christine Blasey Ford.

What would a polygraph test reveal about what might well have been clumsy high school "sexual" interaction? Place that in the context of a sitting Governor routinely engaging in unwanted and unwelcome adult sexual behavior targeting his subordinates.

A case in point, there was former Cuomo aide Lindsey Boylan alleging various instances of sexual harassment and unwanted touching during her tenure in the administration – including, in 2017, Cuomo asked her to play "strip poker" and kissing her on the lips during an encounter in his New York City office. By April 2021, nine accusers had come forward detailing inappropriate actions spanning thirteen years.

Our second group, the deniers, have made it a point to change the topic – to avoid any focus on misconduct by Cuomo; which included his wilful mishandling of the initial Covid-19 infections that researchers have credited for creating the basis for 65% of the American cases.

Cuomo is a level of leader who represents a specific and defined demographic – in Old Testament biblical terms, he is the leader of a Tribe. Those who would lead a nation oversee a tribe but do not directly interfere in its operation – if we were to view it in a Constitutional context, we see states' rights versus federal control. In the Biblical, it was the defining of tribes that had an "inheritance" in the land, and the ruling Levites who had no inheritance but controlled everything.

An interesting aspect of leadership in the context of this second class of followers – the examples given involved conflict and disruption of the normal pattern.

If the herd is peacefully grazing, the method of taking control requires direct conflict with the existing lead stallion – we might find it easier to think of a pride of lions and the one who is their leader.

Because confrontation is messy, we often see those who wish to take power disrupt the peaceful culture. Humans have a thing for creating an enemy, "The Other" who is accused of being a disruptive force. Christians in the Middle Ages and Spain in 1492, focused on the Jews; it didn't matter that they worship a Jew or that the New Testament Bible mandates that they follow Hebrew laws, Jews were educated and prosperous, so they were a natural enemy of the poor.

In 2016 and 2020, we see the animosity directed at the "One-Percent" or the "Elite" class. At the same time, we see laws that favor that group in the area of taxation or a general failure to properly adjust for inflation.

We have welfare subsidizing full-time minimum wage workers – which removes a profit affecting burden from the employers, which then increases the income that escapes taxes and provides a basis for the attack.

Those who want to hold leadership during the stamped know they are a cause of disparities – it's intentional. They also are the root cause of racial inequities. And they know it. They are engaged in intentional acts of creating animosity between various groups. And they can achieve their objectives because there are no True Leaders who can enlighten the masses and so turn the stampeding herd before it runs off a cliff of its own making.

When you create animosity you also create an aspect of the Backfire Effect – fight or flight – and ensure discord that is the basis for assuming leadership in a stampede mentality.

Those trained in debate know they can often win by first agreeing with some aspect of the opposition premise. They then turn the herd by asking if that takes into account certain facts or allows for an alternative interpretation.

Done properly, their opponent will either say no – and in effect admit to a weakness in their position – or go with the alternate premise and possibly concede a some points to the opposing position.

The key point is that a non-confrontational approach will elicit a cooperative response.

Simple phrases, like *"Black Lives Matter,"* can serve to trigger opposition that is made stronger when the alternative, *"All Lives Matter"* is presented and rejected. That opposition grows when the symbol for *"Black Lives Matter"* is a dead drug addict, who died while being restrained by the police.

Then we shift the focus on the police and technique used while downplaying any facts related to the deceased junkie. If done right, the officer or officers involved are punished and we have the basis to call for defunding the police – which will remove law enforcement from the streets and enhance crime in a way that will provide additional fuel to the rhetorical fire.

Those seeking personal benefit from leadership without actually having the responsibilities that go with actually being a leader will focus on disruption. While the second level is in the process of fighting among themselves, these middle-level individuals can quietly gain from their profiteering.

While they seem to have power, they are not true leaders. But, if your goal is personal gain, they are worthy of emulating.

Then we have the third tier – the true leaders.

Third-tier leadership knows how to utilize all the factors that control or disrupt the lower tiers. The primary difference is that they are, by basic nature, leaders. They are the children of the Lion King, of flock leaders, of lead stallions.

YES! As much as we might not want to accept it, they are genetically predisposed to assume leadership positions. More importantly, they were environmentally conditioned to assume the leadership role.

On a general level, we are entering the realm of the most disputed, longstanding, debate topic of *"Nature over Nurture."* Which is more important? Your genetics or the environment in which you were raised and conditioned?

At this point, I should have triggered the Backfire Effect among those who are not natural leaders, thus are generally unsuited for leadership roles. They have experienced both the quest and the frustration of failure – and will spend their lives living with the emotional consequences.

Ideally, assuming they have made it this far, they will stop reading and allow the true leaders to step forward.

Those leaders have probably already realized that the Backfire Effect is being used in this context as a filter – this is a common practice among leaders. It is generally used to focus and control their target demographic.

As with most filters, unwanted particles occasionally get through – so multiple filters are used. In fighting Covid-19, the CDC and Dr. Fauci briefly recommended double masking – and this brings us to a leadership tool or expression that generally works when a leader is dropped into a new situation or needs a quick answer: *"Everything is the same, they just change the name or order of magnitude."*

We draw similes, make analogies, draw attention to the patterns and make a comparison that is sufficiently similar in concept or nature to provide a basis for a tactical solution.

Shakespeare spoke of names in many ways, do we not immediately recognize: *"What's in a name? That which we call a rose, by any other name would smell as sweet."* Yet, without a name, everyone is a nobody and would easily be forgotten.

Those with a knowledge of physics know the electrons in an atom circle a nucellus – the formula and behavior are the same as that which describes planets circling the sun?

A leader sees a similarity, ignores an order of magnitude.

While it might not work in all instances, it is possible and practical to describe the universe with a formula whose order of magnitude varies while the format remains constant.

A leader will utilize similes, metaphors, or accepted basic concepts where changing a single function of magnitude is all that is needed to explain, predict, or control events.

Obviously, they can be wrong, make mistakes, and then be attacked for the errors. But, the real issue is the reason for the "error". It can be something imposed by a rhetorical attack, and therefore is not a true error or lapse in judgment. Or, it can be real and thereby reveal a flaw in the chosen paradigm. This leads us to a classic sign of a good leader – they acknowledge their mistake, learn from it, and move on.

Those who harp on the previous mistakes of others are unsuited to be leaders. When judging someone's past mistakes, the most important observation is whether they were repeated or learned from?

When evaluating your own mistakes, use them as a tool for learning, or as a weapon that will yield some benefit in the future. Regardless, let your errors serve a purpose.

Again, we can turn to the Bible and the use of generally accepted legend or history to make points.

Noah's was a common story whose roots might extend back thousands of years to the end of the Ice Age that flooded the valley which became the Mediterranean Sea. And there was no question that it takes both a male and female to reproduce – hence loading the animals two-by-two.

A fool will quickly accept that the whole world can be placed underwater by rain that falls for forty days – they are a fool because they do not grasp the density of the rain ... that is akin to the output of a high-pressure hose with no air pockets or gaps – water falling at over 100MPh (161KMh) with no air to breath.

As shown in my 2012 book, *"Genesis of Genesis,"* the purpose of the Noah story was actually to break the pattern that defined the timeline created by the 24 patriarchs. Each of the patriarchs was defined by a mathematical formula that gave the age of the current patriarch when the next one was born, and then the number of years the first lived after that birth – as confirmed by their age at death.

The structure created a pattern, a timeline that matched the Hebrew calendar system, and with the story of Noah that pattern was broken and we find the introduction of a three year "Shem Error" which adjusts for an error in the calendar system – akin to that between the Julian and Gregorian systems that occurrent in 1582.

With this example, our leadership point is that one does not argue with accepted mythology or belief, instead, it is used to further the goal of the leaders.

Noah served many such purposes. Consider the idea that

the "men of renown" are said to be the children of the "sons of God" and daughters of men – an immediate acknowledgment and acceptance of the prevailing religious doctrines which were seen in the mythologies of every major culture.

Those familiar with Greek and Roman mythology know what I'm referring to – as would those familiar with the earlier parent religions found China and India.

Symbolically, the flood destroyed a leadership structure symbolized by leaders who claimed divine descent. The prime technique of a leader is to acknowledge their predecessor and then provide a justification for them no longer being in power.

With the Roman acceptance of Christianity, the children of God were unified in Jesus as the only begotten son of God – all others were the sons of divine sons and thus lost their standing.

Once again we face the Backfire Effect – if you attack the previous authority, supporters of that authority will fight back; if you acknowledge and logically supersede that authority, those who support it will sign-on. In the case where there is a "divine right of kings," the process involved eliminating elevation to the status of a god, and instead made them a Saint – same status, different name, and you can still pray to them or ask for their intervention with the more powerful deity.

Again, we see the leaders acting in a non-confrontational way to control the minds of the superstitious while allowing no wiggle room for the naysayers. Rather they allow the naysayer to remain outside the newly evolving doctrine – they can pray to a son of the deity, or the mortal son (grandson of the deity), and thereby exclude themselves from the new power structure.

As we saw with Moses – and is common among Muslims, the Amish, etc – members will dress and groom themselves so that their identity is immediately recognized.

Leaders get their followers to self-identify. That might mean having the followers adopt traits that they must defend.

As we know from history, the Egyptians shaved their hair – it was a form of cleanliness and defense against lice. Hebrews were told not to shave – immediately you create the distinction between the Hebrew and Egyptian. Allowing the sideburns {or *peiyot*} to grow then distinguished Hebrews from other cultures that wore beards.

In some cases, we find warnings, or commonly known – but not publically promoted – realities that must be protected against.

During the Trump Administration, income derived from his Washington D.C. hotel became the basis for calls to invoke the Emoluments Clause of the Constitution. The claim was that the room rentals could be construed to be foreign bribes.

However, Article I, § 9, clause. 8 has a deeper meaning. It is one inferred in my January 2017 book, "Jonathon's POTUS Cousins," and expanded upon in the Trump Card book series.

At the time the Constitution was drafted, and throughout the next 250 years of United Colonies/States history, all of the Presidents have shared a common ancestral line that is shared by the European nobility – since reduced to the British nobility.

Most were cousins to sitting royalty and nobility – which meant they were in line to inherit a title and thus the allegiance to a foreign authority. It also created a situational bias that would allow the open creation of a noble class – a king or the nobility found in a Constitutional Monarchy.

That reality explains why the Constitution states: *"No Title of Nobility shall be granted by the United States: And no Person holding any Office of Profit or Trust under them, shall, without the Consent of the Congress, accept of any present, Emolument, Office, or Title, of any kind whatever, from any King, Prince, or foreign State."*

In April 2021, Britain's Prince Philip died, and among the stories about his life was the often forgotten fact that he had been the child of Danish, Greek, and German Royalty. For him to be the King of England would have passed sovereignty to the other nations, or placed those royal houses under the control of Britain – so when he married Elizabeth, he renounced any-and-all claims he might have had.

The American Constitution had created a renunciation mandate for any who would hold *"any Office of Profit or Trust"* in the colonies that were soon to be designated states.

Historians tell us that within the Continental Army there was an element or individual who wanted George Washington to be designed a King.

The individual in question was Colonel Lewis Nicola who was concerned over the fact that the Articles of Confederation only granted the right of taxation to the States – not the Federal government – and therefore basic funding for military pensions and the support needed for disabled veterans was non-existent.

Thus we have an element of transition faced by leaders in the process of changing systems.

But here we are, 250 years later, the nobility continue to control the powerful nations and those that ousted the nobility are, except for China, the second tier.

When it comes to a debate over *Nature or Nurture*, we can argue a proven continuity of leadership stretching back to the time of Charlemagne (748-814). The continuity in China was broken by Genghis Khan (Temüjin, 1158-1227) and never really recovered.

But leadership is not just control of governments or the basic tribal population, it also dominates public recognition.

In America, many of the top actors and actresses are also descended from Charlemagne. On another level, those who are identified as Indian-Brahmin or Ashkenazi-Levite fall outside that line, but create a parallel line that dates back 6,000 years and is genetically identified as DNA haplotype R1a or J2.

CHAPTER Two - It's as old as History

Leaders learn from their mistakes; occasionally, they fail to learn and repeat the mistakes. Eventually, those mistakes become a personal habit or, if they have sufficient influence, a cultural tradition.

One of the unrecognized fun parts of making mistakes is that there are times when the mistakes are serendipitous – they are happy or beneficial mistakes. Those mistakes are not often seen for what they are – except by a certain type of leader, who will then *"double down."* Spectators don't often know if the *"doubling down"* is a sign of pure stupidity or some form of a strategic approach that will further the leader's goals.

Based on the Old Testament calendar, 9 September 2021 marked Rosh Hashanah, the Hebrew New Year, and transition from the year 5781 to 5782. In those terms, we set the dawn of modern society sometime around the year 3760BCE – Google it, or research history books and academic papers, to see what events were known to have been occurring in that period.

If we adjust for the adjustments that have been made to our Western Calendar, when our year-one was established, it was a reset of the 198th nineteenth year (Metonic) period of the Hebrew Calendar. If you think in terms of a 24-hour military time clock and the civilian 12-hour system which uses AM and PM, you understand why the two systems are the same.

The invention of the Chinese lunar calendar is credited to the first Chinese emperor, Emperor Huangdi, in 2637 BCE – every two hours in a day, month in a year, and year in a twelve-year period, is paired with a zodiac animal. Where the Hebrew is tied to a six-pointed star, the Chinese use a five-pointed one – which has multiple means or uses beyond the five elements of existence: Wood, Earth, Water, Fire, and Metal.

The symbolism attached to calendars was created so that the common person would have something to lock into and give meaning to – first-tier superstition in the form of a zodiac that works because there are patterns of forces that repeat through predictable cycles.

It is only when the environmental factors change that the "magic" vanishes.

For those who do not understand, there was a time when the government could identify the location of "secret" facilities based on the fact that, historically, people seldom traveled more than twenty-five miles from where they were born. A journey of 25-miles was more than an eight-hour walk – five hours by horse. In the old west, the Pony Express would take about three hours, then the rider would need to change horses.

Knowing this, whenever air or early satellite surveillance showed a mass population shift the new location would become "an area of interest." And, if the shift could not be explained in conventional terms – the destruction of a previous settlement or creation of a new commercial operation – the shift generally meant, because it was not in the open, there was a new "secret military-related facility" being created.

Everything of meaning has a reason and often carries a dual purpose. There is a surface or obvious purpose and a Sub-Rosa reality or meaning.

Leaders understand the dual systems and the purpose they serve. A Tier-One individual will have trouble grasping the reality that explains the different representations. Yet, it is as old as history itself. If you see a supposed leader whose premise is irrational, it is likely theat even their most rational seeming assertions are, if implemented, totally crazy – even if sane when implemented by a rational leader.

This means we can go back 6,000-years to the time when the Indus Valley Civilization was taking shape – to a time when the roots of the Indo-European culture were being established. Interestingly, the calendar systems for the Hebrew and Chinese cultures are both Metonic and based on a twelve-month year that is adjusted via the use of the thirteen-month leap year.

Adam appears on the sixth day of the first year. That roughly coincides with the Indus Valley culture and marked the end of early humanities formation. It was an era when humans began to build homes, rather than live in caves.

Of course, we can have anthropological arguments over the stages of civilization or human evolution, but that does not alter the reality of when it all seems to have come together and created what can be termed a foundation of modern civilization and technology.

Google "*Oldest Civilization.*"

The answer is 3000BCE, "*The Sumerian civilization is the oldest civilization known to mankind.*"

The Bronze Age Indus Valley Civilization is dated from 3300 BCE to 1300 BCE. This means the"oldest" criteria would seem to be nuanced.

Throughout this book, you'll be subjected to my habit of cross-referencing to the Bible, and in that context, Adam comes into existence in 3762BCE and dies in 2831 BCE. Therefore, Adam is symbolic of the dawn of civilization and the first two cultures – the first time tribal populations can be identified as something other than "primitive."

Utilizing structures – dated archaeological remains – we can see where and in what sequence early civilizations existed. This also means we have the emergence of leaders in a form we can recognize. We have a date for the birth of wisdom and the beginning of recorded mythology.

In the 1970s, in "*Path of the Serpent,*" I used mythology to trace related cultures; in 2011, a combination of yDNA and that same mythology resulted in "*Grandpa Was a Deity.*" Both books are, indirectly, about leadership. They represent the emergence of leadership in a political-technological context and adhere to genetic lines.

Being a sustained civilization requires a leadership class

that survives across centuries and millennia – this goes beyond the stallion or lion king analogy and gets into the survivability of their offspring and the creation of dynasties.

True leaders create civilizations that have skills, trades, and specialties that serve to differentiate members from their peers; they also create a ruling class that is presented in terms the rest of the classes will accept.

While we have evolved to the point where we can use "social class," in the early cultures there were tribal groups being brought together and had their own oral history identity.

The Bible asserted a common ancestor and identified the Tribes as representing the children of that ancestor's children – this allowed tribal members to view the other tribes as blood cousins.

In India, political unification identified each group based on its functional abilities – this created the basis for the tribal "caste system." The leadership introduced mythology that the story of Noah was intended to end – the primary caste or "Men of Renown" were the grandchildren of Creator Deity.

In India, they were the Brahmin and the Chenchu. The Chenchu were a tribe derived through a mortal mother – the same mythology we see in Hercules, and the biblical *"men of renown"* – later it would be applied to Jesus. But as the origin culture spread to form the other ancient cultures, the same mythology was retasked – along the northern Mediterranean, Hercules provided a common link that relates the origin myths of Greece, Rome, and the Scythians.

One trait that appears to be common among leaders is the ability to rephrase and utilize a core belief of their target demographic. When Christianity became the new religion of the Roman Empire, and as it spread, traditional mythology was rephrased and regional customs were adopted and incorporated into the core belief system. This gave us the Christmas Tree, an Easter Bunny, and an ancient *"men of renown"* origin for Jesus.

In terms of "hard science," the Brahmin and Ashkenazi-Levite are the same yDNA genetic groups – R1a and J2 – and, in India, this can be used to differentiate the various castes and social classes.

In Western culture, we look to the remnants of the Roman and Viking leaders in combination with the Levite and Kohanim. This gives us the descendants of Charles Martel via Charlemagne to the 4-Sisters who are the common ancestors of the American Presidents.

With real-time global communication and a possibility of equal access to intellectual resources, any-and-all "racist" connotations lose their traditional meaning or relevance. With the advent of *Critical Race Theory* an environmentally induced mutation or difference takes on a meaning quite different from the traditional idea of *"Race."*

CRT holds that {1} Race is a social construct, {2} Racism is normal, {3} "interest convergence" control the legal process and all moves toward "equity or equality," {4} stereotypes are fluid and alter with time, {5} all parties fit multiple calcification groups, {6} members of a group are best suited to describe the oppression of that group. The validity of CRT has been called into doubt because it is utilized as a political weapon to be used against "the other" who is defined as having a racial advantage.

Biblical marriage laws recognized tribal differences and held that the average had to marry their own. However, tribal members who showed special abilities could marry into the Tribe's Levite rulers. Their children would then be free to cross the tribal boundary and marry others of the Levite class.

The story of the entry into Israel presents a pattern seen in DNA studies. Invading males are allowed to take indigenous woman but indigenous males are to be killed – that ensures the invader's male genetics will survive and grow in numbers.

YES, this is genetics, or animal husbandry, designed to improve the herd leadership and provide new blood to create a class of elites upon whom those in other regions depend – this is also why the marriage laws forbid marriage to close relatives.

We can look at the early population centers for the more advanced cultures and find there is a geographical justification for many of the locations, and an environmental reason other areas failed to develop – sustainable agriculture and generally "good" weather were primary.

Locations like Britain provided the right location for astrological circles – Stonehenge (3,400 BCE), to the north of which is an Orion Belt layout which we see mirrored in the Great Pyramids. In both locations, the latitude defined the use, and the stones were transported to the appropriate sites.

The leaders were focused on developing cross-generation "scientific" projections. This is something a true leader does – they focus on projects that will enhance knowledge or improve society long after they are gone.

In some instances, like the *Book of Genesis*, there is a mathematical key or pattern that is built into the story that creates the eras or other data.

That key begins with Adam's birth and then follows the pattern: the age the next key child was born; years lived after the birth of a key child; the total number of years (age) at death. The full pattern is in my 2012 book, *"Genesis of Genesis."*

Over time, symbolic references change. The Serpent, and half-serpent woman, along with their tree, were once symbols for Wisdom, Knowledge, and Understanding – they were to be respected and worshiped. Serpent deities are connected to all the astrological-mathematical-based temple construction.

Viewing the ultimate modern symbol of hate, the Nazi swastika, few will realize it was once the universal symbol of Good Fortune or kindness – truly universal because it appears in old and new world cultures. At one time, Jewish households had it on their doorsteps as a sign of good luck; the Mezuzah, with its prayer scroll, would be on the doorpost.

The pentagram, the five-pointed star of China that can be found in ancient Greece and Babylonia is now the Christian sign for the Devil and black magic.

To undermine a culture or knowledge, turn its symbols into things to be feared or hated.

But, ignoring that propagandistic leadership trait, if you wish to be a leader, ask why and how the same symbols and beliefs were present on contents, or in cultures, supposedly geographically isolated from each other. A shorthand dismissal would claim independent discovery lead to the mathematical and mystical patterns being discovered and utilized in the same way by cultures that have no contact.

What does this weird archaeology have to do with a book that talks about leadership?

The New World presents us with a population that is not part of the DNA that dominated the Old World civilizations and cultures. However, a leader or ruling class does not necessarily represent the genetics of the subservient population – we know this from the way Western culture has come to define Eastern or global populations.

Ancient languages were pictographic and evolved into Arabic, Hindu, Hebrew, Chinese, etc. Originally, the Chinese script was written vertically, but because western mathematics requires formulas to be written horizontally, to adopt higher-level mathematics and physics, China shifted its script to a horizontal presentation.

In effect, foreign leadership in science altered what was a founding character of Chinese culture. There was no need for a dominant physical integration – something that, centuries from now, would show in altered DNA patterns. In the case of the Mesoamerican cultures and, by extension, Peruvian society, legends tell of "gods" arriving from the sea, imparting their knowledge in a form that resulted in social change, and then departing.

As discussed in my September 2011 book, *"Grandpa was a Deity,"* we are still using the mythology of leadership that was the root of all advanced civilizations to form or control aspects of the subservient society or population.

In terms of Roman Christianity, it was shifted from a *"Grandpa was a Deity"* basis associated with *"men of renown"* to *"the Deity was his dad"* – and he's the only one who can claim that, so bow to him and all who claim to represent him.

Leaders utilize superstition.

The human mind requires an explanation – that comes with eating from *"the Tree of Knowledge"* and it differentiates humans from other mammal or sentient populations.

One of the primary realizations is that all things have an origin. Logically, when you get to whatever you designate the first thing, you have the problem that – by definition as the first or starting point – it has no origin and, as many ancient wise cultures defined it, is summarized and characterized as a *"self-begotten beginning."*

In terms of our tiers, the *"self-begotten beginning"* – or as often phrased, the eternal or original God – every religion has presented this solution and explanation to those in the first tier population. Every rational person accepts a beginning – at one level, we speak of the universe coming into existence as the result of a *"Big Bang"*, an explosion of pure energy which then degrades into mass as described when $E=MC^2$ is expressed as $M=E/C^2$ – when Energy is decelerated by C^2 (the square of the speed of light).

Leaders understand the science and accept the idea that the terminology applied to the starting point is "GOD" – things need a word or phrase, a simple descriptive term. Those in tier two – the naysayers – will rant against there being a "GOD". In fact, they are saying there is no beginning that does not have a beginning, and therefore, they want to deny science and society of a pragmatic means to designate a point beyond which there is no practical need to seek an origin.

Since science can never reach the origin, "GOD," because both matter and energy exist and interact. You cannot have a state of "pure energy," because there is always matter present – if only as a container or observer.

In biblical terms, you cannot look into the face of God or, it is impossible to reach the beginning. Pure science, pure logic, pure rationality, and everything that the first two tiers are incapable of truly achieving when a third-tier leader is there to control the dynamic or scenario, or whatever. The leader is the one who has a grasp on where things will be - long after they are gone. The good leader sets the stage for growth and benefit, and the bad one might seem worthy but has set the stage for a future disaster – which is the core of Reaganomics.

The Tier Two naysayer claims to be an atheist, which is acceptable when it simply rejects "organized religion." And it is interesting that in America in 2021, membership in a church, synagogue, or mosque is reported was reported to be about 43-percent; in 1937, when Gallup Pollsters first asked people if they *"happen to be a member of a church, synagogue, or mosque,"* the affirmative response was 73-percent.

This tells us that, at least in America, organized religion is going the way of the Pagan Temple.

In the past, "church" attendance represented a positive correlation with physical, mental, and social health. Religion served as the Old Testament designed it to function – it formed a basis for elements of behavior that allowed people to live longer, reduce stress, and relieve symptoms of depression, and, in terms of many dietary or exercise habits, it helped improve cardiovascular and immune function.

For some, the decline in membership among western or organized "Houses of Worship" is seen as a possible negative. But, in many cases, the rigid structure of dictatorial rules has been replaced by "Eastern" religious activities that have given rise to vegan diets which are also associated with addressing climate change, and exercise practices such a yoga.

The idea of worshiping an invisible energy source under the direction of clergy has been replaced by the acceptance of a deity and a focus on personal wellbeing.

Previously, I mentioned how Biblical authors used both existing flood and "grandson of a deity" mythologies in the story of Noah to undermine the existing "pagan" beliefs. Human culture is now transitioning to the next logical stage in its evolution – acceptance of a starting point (called God) and a focus on life over supposed sins with the cries of heresy and the inquisition-style mentality that underlays various forms of bigotry.

With the founding of the United States, Church and State began their separation as a political or social practice. Since it has not become universal, we can expect there will be another "religious war" – something that will pit those who are ruled by religious leaders against those who are now in the process of separating from organized religion.

Here again, we have the point at which third-tier leaders will be making their presence felt.

There will be forces supporting the concept of "religion without organized dictatorial religion" and those who promote dictatorial religion. The religious dictators support the anti-abortion movement by asserting a fetus is a "person" deserving of life, but deny that "person" the status of being counted in a census or having a right to welfare, medical care, or anything that we would normally bestow on a "real" person.

It should be noted that, under New Testament laws, a fetus is the property of the father and there is no law against its destruction. However, if it is not believed to be the husband's child, it is to be aborted, and if it is the husband's child, if it is destroyed (killed) through a third-party attack on the mother, the father must be compensated. But there is no "right to life."

During Prohibition, religious groups attacked alcohol, yet worshiped Jesus – who turned water into wine when there wasn't enough alcohol for the party he was attending. And, of course, the idea of eating pork or shellfish is strictly forbidden – but ignored by those same Bible thumpers when they have their "religious" holiday meals.

When people exit organized religion, they are, in fact, in many ways abandoning the world of rampant hypocrisy.

Leaders understand this and often take advantage of the reality either by promoting the exit or playing to the cognitive dissonance.

A common characteristic of traditional leaders is the use of hatred – attacking "the Other," the one with different beliefs from a different cultural setting.

With the creation of the prevailing form of Christianity, which is based on traditional Roman mythology of the type the "Flood" was supposed to have erased – the idea of leaders as divine-human hybrids – "the Other" became Hebrew or Jewish culture that produced Jesus.

As both history and the New Testament Bible tell us, at first Rome used Herod to undermine the Jewish state – first he married the Israelite Queen, and then when he had sufficient power he killed the sons he had with her. This allowed his other sons to be in line to inherit the throne.

In my September 2012 book, St. Paul's Joke, I show that the timeline and scriptural text supports the idea that Herod might have raped Mary, and the story of him trying to have the resulting son killed would therefore be true – since, as a Jewish woman in the line of King David, who was also related to a High Priest at the Temple, Jesus had a valid claim on the throne; he would have been entitled to the title of, and acceptance as, the King of Israel.

We know that Rome eventually expelled the Jews from Israel and initiated the first century diaspora. This replicated the Assyrian exile that occurred during the 8th century BCE, and we can see it as a pattern that was then repeated by other nations.

On 18 July 1290, King Edward I of England issued an edict that expelled all Jews from his Kingdom – about 350 years passed before Oliver Cromwell would, in 1657, formally permit Jews to return to England. As we know, on 31 March 1492, Isabella I of Castile and Ferdinand II of Aragon issued a joint edict – the Alhambra Decree – which expelled Jews from Spain effective 31 July.

Expulsions have ramifications and for America, the one from Spain triggered funding of Columbus – who set sail on 3 August 1492. As has been covered in other books, because of this, we saw the founding or settlement of Brazil – funded by Jewish merchant families in Portugal.

While Sephardic refugees also went East into Ashkenazi regions, many headed West to the New World and settled in Mexico and on the various Caribbean Islands. In Mexico, the subsequent arrival of the Conquistadors and their defeat of the indigenous Aztec civilization was followed by renewed attacks on the early Jewish settlers – who then went North into what is now California and New Mexico.

As you might have realized, when I mentioned the 350-year expulsion of the Jews from Britain, much of this history is ignored in school textbooks. The rewriting of history, "Cancel Culture," is not new. We grew up with it as a mainstay of our daily lives and learning.

Apart from working historians, only a very small group of leaders are aware of the past. They are very aware of the meaning behind the expression, *"those who are ignorant of history are doomed to repeat it."* However, their motivation is not always avoidance of repetition, rather they are often seeking things that have been shown to work when seeking to control the masses. We need only look to Adolph Hitler to see how the "expulsion" and "diaspora" again came into play.

While the traditional Christian anti-Semitism proved to be highly useful in his rise to power, the universality of it meant that there was no place to expel the Jews to. As we know, when refugee ships headed to the United States, they were quickly turned back – an example was the SS St. Louis which, in May 1939, was turned back and resulted in 620 of its 937 passengers later being returned to Europe, and 254 of them being killed by the Nazis.

Of course, as discussed in Jonathon's POTUS Cousins, if we examine the rise of Hitler, we see he was practicing those doctrines which emerged in post-Civil War America. While the USA did not expel its Jews, at the turn of the century, Harvard University had instituted policies to restrict a growing Jewish enrollment; in 1924, when Hitler's universal best seller, *Mein Kampf*, was published – making him a millionaire – the USA instituted the 1924 Immigration Act, or Johnson-Reed Act, to prevent immigration from Asia and Ashkenazi regions of Eastern Europe.

One of the things Hitler had going for him was the 1917 Russian Revolution – the replacement of the Russian nobility by "*Ones of the Majority*" (Bolsheviks) who emerged in the *Pale of Settlement*, which had been where the Czars had deposited their Jewish population. The key doctrine was drafted by a Jew and the movement was led by Jews along Germany's eastern border. That allowed Hitler to substitute Russia for Jews when talking of a military threat to Germany.

This is how transient power grabs work, you attack those who have a long and established history of retaining their hold on power against superior forces.

After the Second World War, we entered the "Red Scare" period which allowed politicians to adopt Hitler's view of Russia – even though the policies the Russian dictators adopted were destroying their economy. This grew to a frenzy under Joseph McCarthy and McCarthyism – which attacked Biblical socialist doctrines and Hollywood Jews. At the same time, we had the

"Cold War," proxy wars, the Korean Conflict, and Vietnam.

The United States adopted a militaristic posture that now has it allocating, as part of its annual budget, more than that of the next twelve spending nations. Through that budget and other spending, America now subsidizes most of its economic competitors. Most important is the fact that the military has taken on an aggressive tactical policy – when it is a retaliatory defensive posture that would be the most beneficial.

We have our past, and now we have the Biden era.

There is a pandemic with annual deaths are comparable to that associated with smoking and second-hand smoke; there is a strong movement for economic change with elements that have already been enacted in response to the pandemic; there is also a resurgence of the classic response to "Others."

The southern borders of America and many European nations are faced with the anticipated climate change migration problem. Those wishing to capitalize on the propaganda that is associated with differences have taken to yelling xenophobia and racism where the real issue is one of national health and economic security.

There are few nations (if any at all) that can sustain a massive non-productive population increase; fewer can handle the biological adaptation required to deal with the introduction of foreign diseases. In 1892, the United States opened Ellis Island as an immigrant screening site and port of entry.

As has been reported, in 2021 Covid-19 infected migrants from South American were crossing into the United States. And we have no idea what indigenous tropical diseases they might be carrying because they are immune – an immunity that does not exist in the Northern Hemisphere.

However, that concern is not one that will gain traction in the media, so we can look to the fallback classic discussed in the previous paragraphs.

In April 2021, there was an article in which we were

presented with the words of Evangelical Christian Pastor Rick Wiles as presented on his *'TruNews'* show. We learned that he was preaching that America is "*under the bondage of satanic spirit*" which wants to destroy Russia because the Bolsheviks overthrew the Russian monarchy, and seven years later were overthrown by the anti-Semitic founders of what we know as Russian Communism.

As Pastor Wiles was said to have stated: "*The reason the ruling deep state of America hates the Russian people and wants to destroy them?   It is the satanic Zionist power that overthrew the Russian government in 1917, did a human blood sacrifice of the Romanov family – a satanic ritual where they slaughtered the Romanovs, it was a satanic blood sacrifice – that same group of Satanists that overthrew the Russian people in 1917, that's what controls America today. That spirit right there is what is destroying the United States of America, destroying our freedom, destroying our culture – that spirit right there.*"

Look at the classic buttons: a ritual involving a Satanic Blood Sacrifice – this is the classic "Blood Libel" that has been popular since the middle ages; a Zionist-Jewish charge related to the killing of the Romanov family, but also one that ignores the fact that, after the 5 May 1789 revolution, the French guillotined all their core nobility, only to later see the rise of a higher form of nobility in the ascent of Emperor Napoleon Bonaparte.

While attacking what he calls Zionist Jews, Wiles made it a point to cover himself by saying: "*Who attacks us? Who's always attacking us? Zionists. There's nobody else attacking me. Zionists. It's not every Jewish person, it's the Zionists. It's the satanic Zionists. They are satanic.*"

Apparently, both "us" and "me" are those being attacked – so it becomes Wiles and his followers who are being attacked by Jewish satanic forces. By definition, Zionist and Zionism is a reference to the Hebrew speakers and movement to recreate a Jewish presence in Israel. Thus the Satanic forces are those who seek to reinstate Israel – something predicted in the Book of Revelation to occur in the twentieth century, or during what is his lifetime.

Apparently, Wiles is addressing people who are willing to accept these Zionists "*...want war with Russia because the Russian people got free of their chains and bondage and returned to Christ. That's what it's about. The Russian people returned to Christ.*" Of course, if there was such a return to Christianity, it occurred after the 1991 fall of the Soviet Union.

Wiles also alleged that the Federal Government had been stockpiling bullets and guns which were to be used "*to round up Christians and constitutionalists under a President Hillary Clinton.*" Thus, it would appear that Trump's victory saved Christians from the fate suffered by Jews during the Holocaust.

Instead, Wiles has bemoaned the failure of the Trump administration to "*put the hollow-point bullets to good use and get out there and put down this communist revolution so the rest of us can live our lives peacefully.*" Defined as part of the American communist revolution were those supporting *Black Lives Matter.*

Pastor Wiles is a low-level individual playing the classic game designed to attract Tier One individuals with the lowest functional IQ.

However, his use of the Russian Revolution introduces something we've touched on before – nations lose their status upon their break with the 4-Sisters or its traditional Nobel line of control over European affairs.

In 2018, Prince Philip's mitochondrial DNA was utilized to positively identify the Romanov remains. Prince Philip who was husband to Queen Elizabeth, and designated The Duke of Edinburgh, was the great-nephew of Empress Alexandra, the wife of Tsar Nicholas.

CHAPTER Three - Learn to Think

One difference between a leader and a follower is found in the ability to think. Leaders are marked by their utilization of the herd's inability to think rationally, its visceral reaction to anything considered threatening to its safety.

Those who use religion as a tool for taking power are the first to emphasize the elements to be feared – Hell, Satan, the threat of eternal damnation, and punishment. Other religions us the positives – spiritual enlightenment, tranquility, and peace in an environment or state-of-being of love.

Play with the Western definition of GOD: All-knowing, all-wise, infallible, perfect, and eternal.

The beauty is that religious power brokers know their flocks are too dim-witted to think about the definition of that deity. They also ignore the character of the world around them – how balanced and perfectly imperfect it is. There is no waste; all things are recycled; the conservation of energy is a guiding scientific principle.

We have the nonsense argument that says there is no God, yet says things are eternal – which is the core definition of God. Gee, everything is the same, they just change the name – then argue against that which they argue for, but only because they don't like the name you selected for what they revere.

Is the Universe eternal? Will energy and matter always exist? If not, where would they go to?

If it is eternal, then it is God. So God exists. If there is mathematically "perfect," then it is "perfect." If there is a basis for asserting the possibility of a Unified Field Theory, then you are seeking the "All-knowing" formula defining all of creation – you seek God's All-knowing basis or thought. God exists.

Energy {E} equals Mass {M} moving at the speed of light squared {$E=MC^2$}. The formula is a conversion recipe. Stop all motion and you have Mass without Energy.

But, What if the formula was M=E/C2? If C=zero, all the motion or energy is within the mass.

In mathematical science, anything divided by zero yields an answer of infinity; so you get infinite Mass and zero external Energy. All apparent energy is internal to the Mass.

Mass is nothing more than atoms; atoms are electrons in motion around a nucleus. Mass is defined by its atoms. Energy is motion and the two serve to define existence. Moreover, the formula makes it impossible for them to cease existing – they are eternal. They are "God." Leaders understand this, and by arguing rhetoric or definitions deniers deny reality.

Everything requires a starting point – an origin – and if we decide that the starting point which has been labeled God is impossible, then all we call existence is also impossible.

Leaders understand that God is irrelevant to existence – "*Cogito, ergo sum,*" is the Latin phrase used by René Descartes which expresses the ultimate conclusions: "*I think, therefore I am.*" And as he explained it, "*we cannot doubt of our existence while we doubt.*"

Rational thought dictates while we exist, so does God. While we are not necessary for existence, we can hold that God exists, while there is existence.

During the pre-historic period, Neanderthals evolved an explanation for their existence – they invented deities, and the earliest we can identify was the Serpent, Tree, and woman, who were all associated with Wisdom. That association is universal among all the subsequent civilizations.

A primary characteristic of good leadership is to provide a simple explanation that can be used as a framework for the advancement of society and culture.

The Garden of Eden story tells us that, like any common "pet," Adam could obey. But before the Serpent convinced Eve the Apple was safe, Adam could not think.

The Serpent was created to enlighten Eve, who then gave

the fruit of wisdom to Adam.

There was no original sin, other than the disobedience of an illogical command – to not eat one form of the only food Adam was directed to eat exclusively. Eve was there to elevate Adam to a new level, with the Serpent as a messenger.

Eve did not sin – she helped God elevate Adam to a plain that was higher than a base animal.

Even when asserting creation mythology, those who cannot think, tend to accept things that do not conform to their definition of creation – are not part of the design – many errors and imperfections created by a perfect deity. They cannot grasp that the world, the universe, only functions because it is out of balance – it is perfectly out of balance; it is perfectly imperfect.

Think about the Garden Story: Adam was commanded to only eat fruits and vegetables – but was specifically told not to eat only one of them, and when he obeyed the rules, he was presented with a mate who was not told the rule, and a talking creature was created who could use logic to get Eve to violate the rule we saw Adam obey.

All the ancient cultures assign Wisdom to the female who is often depicted as half-serpent. Drop her into the sea and you get a seductive Mermaid whose song overcomes the normal programming of the male brain and entices him to change his behavior.

Ancient Hercules, a hero revered in myth, legend, and TV or movie plots, was the son of the God *Jupiter* and the mortal *Alcmene* – making Hercules one of the men of renown in the days before Noah's Flood.

One of the legends associated with Scythians – deemed by the Greeks to be the Wisest of all people – is that their first king was Scythes, the son of Hercules and the half-woman-half-snake, *Echidna*. The wisest of people are descendants of a man created by a deity matched to a woman connected to a serpent – the Garden of Eden story.

When the Roman Empire adopted Christianity, Hercules and the other *"Men of Renown"* were unified and redefined as Jesus – a boy whose true father was never mentioned; one who was raised by, and took the name of his adopted father. As with Hercules, Jesus became *"Man of Renown."*

Why do people insist on keeping variations on the same mythology alive and treating it as if it were true?

How do leaders make use of that human trait?

Do they attack and trigger a backfire effect, or do they go with the flow, run to the head of the stampeding herd, and then, when they are recognized as the leader, do they lead them to a safe pasture? Or to the slaughterhouse?

Are Palestinians establishing a prosperous community, or are they devoting their resources to harming their neighbor?

Philosophically, humans like to interpret things in terms of good and evil while insisting that both are under the control of a single *"all-knowing-all-powerful entity"* which, logically, should be able to foresee and prevent anything it doesn't want or that does not comply with its overall *"plan."*

Consider the eons of humans who have accepted magical figures at face value; consider the number of Americans who vote based on that belief system. If you wish, we can generalize the pattern and see it play out in the 9-11 suicide attacks and all the other suicide murders that define and characterize Middle Eastern culture.

Alternatively, you can shrug your shoulders and dismiss anything that ties back to traditional patterns of thought and belief which have served to shape evolution and currently can be seen shaping American society.

Historically, humans do not take responsibility for their actions or decisions.

In recent years, leaders have exposed that reality in ways that serve their ends – in November 1969 many heard Richard Nixon say: *"to you, the great silent majority of my fellow*

Americans – I ask for your support."

His *"Silent Majority"* was the herd that follows where others lead and declines to express any opinion they are not told to have – while he stands naked before them, they are willing to see the Emperor's New Clothes.

The *"Silent Majority"* is defined by those who decline to vote and then complain about the outcome of the election.

People find it easy to ignore what is blatantly obvious – *"the elephant in the room"* – and, when told to, they welcome any opportunity to complain. Both Leaders and MSM realize this and play to it in different ways.

POTUS-45, Donald J. Trump, built a career by forcing MSM to look at him. Trump positioned himself to be a media symbol or icon, and when he became President he restructured his image so the media would continue to mention him.

Granted, in 2017, that involved 89% of the focus being negative coverage, and only 11% positive {according to a Media Research Center study}.

With POTUS-46, Joseph R. Biden, we have an individual who "hides in his basement," who is a politician and therefore avoids media coverage of the type summarized by PT Barnum: *"I don't care what the newspapers say about me as long as they spell my name right."*

Trump is Barnum, and Biden certainly is not – meaning MSM has less to work with. That means it pays MSM to attack Trump and overlook worse conduct from Biden.

Biden can move through his self-inflicted border crisis; he can openly oppose Senator/President Obama's Secure Fence policy; he need not fear the media enlightening the public. But, just in case, he placed Kamala Harris in charge and allowed her to become the target of any "bad press."

Is there a Garden of Eden analogy? Is America as the forbidden fruit, with the Illegals as Adam after Eve {Biden} and the Serpent {Pelosi} pronounced it safe to come?

Pelosi and other long-term elected Democrats have held firm to their support of Ronald Reagan's 1980 open border and amnesty stance. But when Democrat Obama was in office, they could not afford to overtly oppose him.

It was awkward.

But then Trump won the Oval Office and suddenly they could openly oppose Obama by opposing Trump. They could even blame Trump for policies and conditions that were set in place under Obama.

Illegals are warm bodies, with no pathway to citizenship or voters rights, who are counted in the census and determine the representative allotment – but they have no political voice.

For context, the 2020 Census established the American population has grown by 7.4% – the second slowest growth rate in the nation's history. The Experts attribute this to a number of factors involving an aging population, slowing immigration, and the Great Recession of 2007-2009.

With Covid-19 culling the elderly, the growth rate should slow even more. This is especially true since Generation-X, the Baby-Bust generation assures negative population growth with a pattern of delaying both marriage and families. The birthrate is half of that needed for "replacement" and less than a third of what is needed for growth.

In 2020, the number of people over eighty years old was equivalent to the number of children under the age of two. And both numbers will be falling more.

Based on the 2020 Census statistics, roughly a third of the population is under 21-years old, and slightly more are over the age of 55. Given the anticipated life expectancy and the low birthrate, and allowing for normal deaths among the younger age groups, in thirty years the American population should be about a third lower than the 331,449,281 Census total.

This is annoyingly consistent with the Book of Revelation assertion that a third of life will die by the middle of the 21st century – by 2050. That "third of all life" is strengthened by the heat-induced death of millions of sea creatures combined with the extinction of many land animals and various forms of plant life.

The projection entails no magic or superstition. in terms of the Bible, it does reflect an understanding of natural cycles connected to a Metonic {19-year} calendar system. The dating was presented in *"Biblical Prophecy: Are we in the Revelation Era"* and published by Amazon in 2014.

In theory, a variation on the Unified Field Theory which balanced resources against reproduction and added in climate change effects with disease spread would yield the projection. And, in recent history, we can see that projection reflected in books like "The Population Bomb" which invoked a few of the Revelation triggers – famine, disease, pestilence – at a time when the world was focused on nuclear holocaust and war.

When Stanford University Professor Paul R. Ehrlich was writing his book, there were only 3.5 Billion people in the world – in 2021 that number is approaching 8 Billion – and he did not see technological wherewithal to continue to feed the growing population. The fact is, the population had almost doubled from where it was, in 1932, when he was born.

But the universe is perfectly imperfect and utilizes that to keep itself in balance. Accordingly, we have Climate Change – while it threatens sea-level rise that will flood many areas, it is also tuning cold climates warm and snow into rain, with the result that new agricultural areas are being created – such as the Siberian region of Russia and adjoining border areas shared by China.

As I've pointed out in numerous books, when you make a chart of population and global warming, the two curves are synchronized. By melting permafrost, global warming creates agricultural land which can then, if we focus on be vegans – as Adam was told to do – do not eat any food derived from animals and do not use other animal products, so do not need to raise animals to provide those products, eliminating one of the things known to contribute to global warming.

We need to learn to think.

Magic or religious hogwash? Nope, just things we know people knew at the time when the Bible was being written.

In a subsequent chapter, I will be quoting Socrates in the context of the same words appearing in the New Testament and being attributed to Jesus – who lived 400 years after Socrates. It's the "Golden Rule" which appears in the Hebrew Testament as Leviticus 19:33/4 and might well apply to America in 2021 – "*When a foreigner resides among you in your land, do not mistreat them. The foreigner residing among you must be treated as your native-born. Love them as yourself,...*"

That does not mean "*carte blanche*" acceptance. Rather it refers to those who openly and honestly come to reside in your land – who are there legally, not as miscreant thieves or other criminals entering your home. Though, it still applies to the extent that you would treat them as you would any native-born miscreant.

A population decline implies both a worker shortage and a need for automation and technologies that reduce reliance on manual labor or warm bodies. Immediately we know we need to replace welfare – have a UBI – to reduce the workforce that currently administers welfare-related services. If every voting-age citizen receives a poverty level UBI, welfare can end – and the related costs will be significantly reduced.

Social Security ceases to be "Insurance" and continues as earned pension benefit associated with for working – payments to Social Security are derived from all earned income, the idea of a cap on income subject to contributions must end.

Current economic issues are connected to a population decline. But, people ignore the fact that they are creating the decline because of the attitude they express toward those they often call "Welfare Queens."

Learn to think. Learn to make connections. If people should not have children they cannot afford, but they cannot afford the children because the minimum wage is insufficient to maintain a household – requiring a welfare subsidy – nobody can afford children. That means when the condom breaks the result of fertilization becomes abortion.

But the same people who oppose abortion are those who oppose raising the minimum wage, providing both pre and postnatal medical care coverage, and subsequent childcare that would allow the parent to return to work.

The move toward early learning – having children enter pr-school at age three or four – helps address the child care issue, and serves to ensure a better prepared modern workforce. And, in terms of education, it has been realized that, just as we once found High School was necessary, we now see two or four-year free community college educations are necessary to meet the demands of modern culture and economic survival.

If the cost of childcare – the cost of having someone care for your child while you work – is too expensive, economically, it is irrational for a parent to work, or for someone who would like to have a career to also plan to have children.

We hear that UBI means people will not work. But that also means those people who continue working want to work, earn, prosper, and they will be more diligent. It also means the creative can devote their time to their creativity – and thus can have the future profit it could generate.

The Covid-19 Stimulus Checks established that providing money supports the basic economy and expands the broader one associated with a broad-based financial market expansion – increased stock values. If the cap were removed on income subject to Social Security contributions, more than ten percent of all earned income would serve to support the UBI system and provide Social Security Benefits.

The UBI would be both universal for all citizens, and tax-exempt. We should also go back to making Social Security tax-exempt – taxing it disincentives working beyond a certain level.

As it stands, in 2021, income above $142,800 is exempt from the SSI contribution tax – this exempts the wealthy from properly contributing, while double taxing it when they retire.

We promote rules that contradict the alleged purpose of those rules. It is a case of "GOD" creating Eve because Adam was willing to obey the rules and stay ignorant.

Adam, like every base creature, was created to obey the rules and not think about them. But, obviously, from the very beginning, that was not the "purpose of the plan."

With the Serpent – the traditional giver of wisdom and tree that was its source – the ancients envisioned a grand design that used the acquisition of the benefits that define humanity – wisdom, knowledge, and understanding – would also instill another benefit, the sense of guilt, of error, of a need to correct one's actions so that you learn from them.

The authors of the Old Testament were wise enough to realize that a sense of right and wrong cannot be 'taught' in the way an understanding of the calendar could be. We learn to improve by understanding what we did wrong – the same way we learn to ride a bike or learn to play some game or sport.

If we did not have a visceral and basic fundamental idea of personal error we would not have the notion that *practice makes perfect*" but some errors cannot be undone – especially when they involve violating basic rules. Thus, before we violate "tradition," it is necessary that we understand the context in which that tradition arose – we must understand the reason for its existence.

When the reason no longer exists – ceases to be relevant to the times – we must adapt to the new reality. For a leader, that does not necessarily mean discarding the tradition, but it does mean that it can be augmented or serve as the basis for establishing a new tradition.

Few people realize the beauty of the Book of Genesis – it begins and ends on the same note, under the same conditions.

In Verse 1 of Chapter 1, we are told *"God created the heaven and earth."* And the *"the spirit of God hovered over the face of waters."* Then, the next few verses speak of *"waters"* and the creation of "light", with the definition of night and day – verse 5 ends with the first day being declared.

On the second day, the waters are divided and we have the firmament – identified as heaven – being created between the water above and below. Then, on day three, the water below gathers together, then parted and the dry land is called earth.

So, immediately, we learn that a day in our calendar is not a creation day in biblical terms – our day is the rotation of the earth on its axis, and the earth was created on the third day. Thus, creationists have no basis for asserting their earth-day-based timeline. They cannot even declare a "heavenly" day as the basis, since "heaven is a firmament within the waters and the creator, and its concept of a day, is outside of the waters.

If we think in scientific terms, the creator is on the other side of "The Big Bang" and the Bible is describing that event in terms of light, dark, and water (Hydrogen-Oxygen or H2O).

On the fourth day, we get the sun and seasons – the orbit of the earth and its motion on its axis – which is accompanied by the emergence of plants. We are told that on the third day the sun is created to rules the day, the moon to rule the night.

Animal and marine life come into existence on the fifth day – and remember, this is still a divine, pre-Big Bang day. It is on the sixth day that we get genetic reproduction associated with animals, and after that, a man emerges.

A basic sequence of evolution is held and remains intact.

The first six days describe evolution in terms of days that are measured in millions of our years. And then, with the story of the Serpent, the chronological system ends and the oldest known representation of the connection between the Serpent,

Women, and the Tree of Knowledge is formally acknowledged.

We start, 4.5 billion years ago, with 'earliest earth' and then move to 'water' and on through an equivalent of six bible verse steps until we get to the earliest apes {Adam}.

The science we know today was written more than two thousand years ago, possibly three thousand.

Of course, that should not surprise those who can think. We know the battery existed in that period, as did the use of hydraulics to move things or open doors "magically." And we still have not fully figured out how they moved the megalithic stones to create Stonehenge and the pyramids – why we need tractors or cranes to do what they did with nominal manpower.

In "*Genesis of Genesis*", I showed the math that defined the generations from the end of the first chronological system to Noah – when the formula is broken by *the Shem Error* that is matched to, or synchronized to, the Flood. And here is the beauty of what is never mentioned but is presented clearly.

The Bible story of Creation extends from divine moments before the Big Bang and an existence that is defined by water, darkness, and light – then extends to the mythical Flood which also was supposed once again cover the world with water. It was the point in time when we were to bring an end to the divine connection that defined "*Men of Renown.*"

The structure of the text begins and ends on identical conditions – earth that has its firmament underwater in a universe where the firmament called heaven was created from dividing water. And, after the mathematical linkage ends with Shem, when the chronology continues, the defining point for Moses and the Exodus is, once again, the parting of the water.

Symbolically, the parting of the waters and emergence of dry land is presented as marking a transition point. But, isn't it curious – the mirror image of parting waters is rising. When Pharoah's forces attempted to pursue Israelites, the water was returned to cover the land. And now we are in the era of Global

Warming where waters are again rising to cover the firmament we call earth/soil. An era of change is sweeping the earth.

Moses had the role of introducing new dietary and health laws – codes of behavior that further a healthy society, where health involves a code of personal and social behavior which serves to further the general health and welfare of the society.

Leaders phrase things in terms the herd can accept.

Throughout European history, we can see plagues spread because basic {Biblical} health practices were violated.

When we hear talk about Climate Change, we also hear assertions about the degree to which our meat-based diets are contributing to the problem.

When the Black Plague took over Europe, what was the normal attitude to bathing; was there an abundance of garbage for rats, and a marked absence of cats – who were associated with witches, with those same alleged witches or practitioners of herbal medicine, being blamed? And wasn't it the good health enjoyed by the "witches" that proved they had cursed those who were sick?

Tier one mentality is consistent throughout history.

Look at Covid-19. Isn't its origin associated with pork or meat markets in China? And, when we look at the fatality rate, we are told there were mitigating circumstances caused by pre-existing medical conditions – the obese and elderly who spent their lives following unhealthy behavioral practices comprise the fatality numbers.

But, as the CDC numbers presented in the last two books of the Trump Card series show, the number of Covid deaths simply replaced deaths that would have been reported in one of a dozen other categories tracked weekly by the CDC.

While we are looking back to the 12 volume Trump Card series, it is worth noting that it consistently called for various reforms; if we now look to President Biden's first address to Congress, we see these same reforms referenced above.

Those who followed my 12 volume Trump Card series – published during the Trump administration – are aware of the various economic policies the books promoted. In his first address to Congress, given on 28 April 2021 – the 99th day of his administration – Biden recognized House Leader Pelosi and Senate Leader Schumer to announce, *"Together — we passed the American Rescue Plan."* {ARP}

With more than a third of the population vaccinated, Biden had already met and exceeded that first 100-days goal in the war against Covid-19. Now he was explicitly calling for:

1. ARP to place *"on track to cut child poverty in America in half this year."*

2. ARP proposed *"a once-in-a-generation investment in America itself."* Its goal to improve infrastructure and possibly address contributing causes of Climate Change, contaminated water, and other issues affecting the next generation.

3. Acknowledging that *"good-paying jobs that can't be outsourced,"* Biden also pointed out that these jobs are Blue-collar. With that he also stated, *"Wall Street didn't build this country. The middle class built this country. And unions build the middle class."*

4. Adding, as a planned afterthought, *"By the way – let's also pass the $15 minimum wage. No one should work 40 hours a week and still live below the poverty line."* But that is not ARP, it is something called the Paycheck Fairness Act.

5. Finally, Biden made it clear that, in America, *"We will see more technological change in the next 10 years – than we saw in the last 50 years."* But we know that, it was in the first two books of the Trump Card series, published in 2017 when it was pointed out that Trump's objective was to reclaim what had been outsourced to China – resulting in them having what has proved to be a technological leader in many areas. As America and the World heard Biden acknowledge, *"we're falling behind in that competition. ...China and other countries are closing in*

fast."

6. Four years earlier, Trump suggested Solar collectors be installed along the southern border – the idea was dismissed. Now, Biden has recognized *"We have to develop and dominate the products and technologies of the future: advanced batteries, biotechnology, computer chips, and clean energy."*

Good and necessary ideas don't care about politics – but, the reality is that politics often serves to delay the expansion of those ideas into a normal part of daily life.

While he recognized that, short-term, most new jobs will be blue-collar, Biden also pointed out that *"access to a good education"* is one of the *"biggest challenges facing American families today."*

As he pointed out, "When this nation made 12 years of public education universal in the last century, it made us the best-educated and best-prepared nation in the world. 12 years is no longer enough today to compete in the 21st Century."

Of course, we have people in Tier One and Two who like ignorance. For some, it means they are part of the majority, but others see it as a way to have slaves without formal slavery.

Biden proposed *"two years of universal high-quality pre-school for every 3- and 4-year-old in America"* to which *"we add two years of free community college."* This can then be augmented by Pell Grants and scholarships which would be available to four or more year curriculums.

As Biden credited to the First Lady, *"any country that out-educates us is going to out-compete us."* And again, in the Trump Card series, it was pointed out that China sends its best and Brightest to America to learn, then they return home and use that learning to become Billionaires using that knowledge against America.

Isn't strange that bad-and-nasty Communist-Socialist nations have proved to be more Capitalistic than America; have created more Billionaires in a generation. But then, in the case of China, we are talking about people who have been Capitalists since the time of the Rome Empire and the dawn of what would become the Silk-Road that gave rise to paper money.

Comically, some might have recognized Biden expressing a lesson my father taught me, one which I have cited numerous times in my books: *"When they knock you down, make sure you get up, then knock them down, and make damned sure they do not get up."*

For my father, it was a lesson learned as a bare-knuckle boxer, a child old enough to understand the first world war and the influenza pandemic that followed – then he worked his way through Law School, passing his BAR exam concurrent with both his 21st-birthday and the onset of the Great Depression.

Biden made 'Life" our opponent and nationalized it: *"Life can knock us down. But in America, we never stay down. In America, we always get up."*

Of course, since all credit and blame stops at the Oval Office, Biden took credit for the economy creating *"1.3 million new jobs in 100 days"* and *"The International Monetary Fund is now estimating our economy will grow at a rate of more than 6% this year."*

But those who know how to think know the numbers are the normal response to a recession of the type caused by a virus and not real economic factors. They saw the same records set between the 1918 Pandemic and 1929 Crash – whoever is in the Oval in 2031 might also see a Stock Market or Cryptocurrency Crash of historic proportions.

That is, if an observed 11-year economic or business cycle pattern is sustained in what might emerge to be a new "work from home" economy. Keep in mind, the economic crash under Bush ended in 2009 and the Covid-19 pandemic was perfectly timed to create a crash eleven years later, in 2020.

The economy was artificially suppressed by the call for lockdowns, but that only helped expand the new economy that is based on online shopping and home delivery. We saw a sharp change in the entertainment industry – again, with the 1900's "go-to" theaters being replaced by online premium viewing and streaming services.

The economic waters were parted, allowing society to cross into a new era. In terms of theater or entertainment, the gypsy became the roadshow or tent circus; the roadshow gave way to the theater and that became the silent movie house and then the home of "talkies"; of to the side we saw the emergence of radio with its audio dramas; then came television, cable and now streaming through the air or new standard telephone line.

Learn to think. Times change. Cultures change with the exposure to new ideas, or the expanded distribution of old ones.

As a leader, Biden emerges from his basement to express all the right ideas, to expose all the buttons we should push. He denounced the nonsense of Reaganomics and the Trickle-Down idea which supported outsourcing.

He declared it was time to grow the economy the way economies naturally grow: *"It's time to grow the economy from the bottom up and middle-out."*

He also bent to politics, he mentioned George Floyd and praised the verdict. But while he was doing that, the media was releasing data on the death of a California Latino man who died under circumstances to Floyd.

Interestingly, the death occurred concurrently with the beginning of jury deliberation in the Chauvin case, And while being held down on the ground, George Floyd took 9 minutes to die, it only took 5 minutes for a California police officer to kill Mario Gonzalez in a similar fashion.

Thus, with the Chauvin verdict, it would be reasonable to charge the California officer with murder. Or, to use Biden's words, *"After the conviction of George Floyd's murderer, ... – if we have the courage to act,"* we have a case that has set a clear precedent for the future treatment of all police acting in the line of duty.

As Biden told Congress and the World, "*We have all seen the knee of injustice on the neck of Black America.*" So now we need to see if he feels the same way about Latino America – do their lives have value?

Biden wanted police reform legislation passed by the first anniversary of George Floyd's death. But how will it reform the police and the way those resisting arrest are subdued?

It's important to ask questions and think about whether the answers conform to the question.

All too often we either see the premise ignored, or don't even consider it when reacting to a statement. We saw this with the "Original Sin" analysis, where the "All-knowing" entity or source demonstrated it did not "Know" the ramifications of its combined decree and acts.

Thinking about the story allows us to take another view.

Using my premise that the universe evolved in a manner that makes it perfectly imperfect, Adam was intended to eat from the tree. But his obedience showed he was "too perfect," and the Serpent was sent to correct that.

The story is an allegory that continues to be explored in the repeated emphasis on the importance of scholarship to the evolution of humanity and its society. We are pounded over the head with the premise – the spirit of "god" is found in "Wisdom, Knowledge, and Understanding."

In the cultural-economic structure, it is the solemn duty of the merchant to support the scholar and their families.

In practice, we see "socialist" nations having the highest tax rates – in order to pay for that support and all other basic needs. Yet, when we look at net disposable incomes after those costs are paid, we see those socialist nations have more money than their American counterparts. Think! Ten dollars more in taxes saves you a hundred in insurance premiums.

CHAPTER Four - *TARGET YOUR AUDIENCE*

Practitioners of hypnosis are aware of two cardinal rules which might seem contradictory:

1. When hypnotized, a person will not do anything they would not normally do. And,

2. When hypnotized, a person will do anything.

Though contradictory, both are true.

Those who can think, realize why both rules hold. And that the difference is in the phrasing used by the hypnotist.

It is rather basic – though shalt not kill, yet you can kill to defend yourself from being killed.

The reality is the context, phrasing, and/or format of the instruction/command.

The unifying rule is "*You can get anyone to do anything if you phrase it correctly.*"

Who is your target audience?

If you properly define your audience, you can learn what they will accept and then phrase things accordingly.

We've all seen and experienced it. Donald J. Trump has persistently been attacked for being highly skilled at defining and speaking to his target demographic.

A common attack on Trump is his speech pattern. Thou what is commonly ignored is the fact that it resonates with his base. They relate to it. He's a billionaire who speaks as they do, and this tells his demographic that they too can achieve a level of success. They can "Make America Great Again."

Trump's detractors make it a point to assert the fact he inherited the resources which served as the foundation for his real estate empire.

In an attempt to undermine his hopeful image, they also point to his failures, the ventures that went broke. But this is a context lie, and Atlantic City is a prime example.

Trump entered Atlantic City at a time when Reservation Indians were first creating legalized gambling casinos, and the New Jersey authorities saw gambling as a means of revitalizing Atlantic City. Trump was among the first to see the potential.

However, when he was divorcing his first wife, he folded the operation – walking away with $40 million in tax shelter benefits to be applied to his other income.

Detractors yell failure. But those with intelligence look at the events that followed – unable to compete with a growing number of casinos throughout the Northeast, Atlantic City went broke. It appears, Trump saw what was coming and closed his operation while it could still return a cash flow profit – and save him some money in the divorce settlement.

As graduate school accountants are taught, bankruptcy is a profitable form of tax planning. One of the most famous examples was the collapse of the New York real estate leverage operation of William Zeckendorf Sr. In 1965, his bankruptcy became legendary. What is never mentioned is that his family remained wealthy; the overall effect on their monetary situation was negligible.

Naysayers tend to obscure the reality they created. It is a sad truth that those who attack Trump are doing so because he is better at their game than they are. They want to define the rules and get angry when someone else understands those rules – comprehends their true intentions or objective.

As a Republican, Trump's audience is moralistic – they were the anti-slavery party of Lincoln. The Democrats were the pro-slavery deceivers of men who used scripture to justify their immorality. With their defeat, the Democratic leadership was unable to continue their deception and became atheists – which attracted the Socialist 48ers and restructured American politics.

Moralists are hypocrites; their scripture reveals the full extent of that hypocrisy. I use Western scripture, but since *"The*

Golden Rule" is universal, Buddhist, Hindu, or Muslim texts reveal similar things. Atheists have neither a moral code nor any objective standard, but they are consistently inconsistent in their advocacy and a leader takes that under consideration.

Consider a common reality among the Pro-Life groups – those who oppose abortion because the fetus is a person and abortion is murder. They no abortion under any circumstances – and, until the Supreme Court stepped in, that included saving the life of the mother. Supposedly the Bible is on their side.

It sounds good.

But then we introduce a tubular pregnancy where both mother and fetus will die. Pro-Lifers argued the mother's death was "God's Will" and OK if their rules result in the death of both mother and fetus. Rather than save one, they kill two.

They oppose the use of contraception and advocate that abstinence is the only "moral" method; their book commands they should be fruitful and multiply – making abstinence a sin.

If the woman wanted children, her death would mean no future children would be produced. Therefore we can assert the Pro-Life groups not only are willing to murder the mother, but they are also preemptively murdering the potential children.

The only applicable Biblical reference for their position states that a violent attack on a pregnant woman, which causes the loss of the fetus, means the husband shall receive financial compensation in an amount that he deems acceptable {Exodus 21:22-25}.

A fetus is not a person, it has neither "birthright" nor name {independent identity}. Biblically, personhood connects to the birthrights granted when a fetus emerges naturally from the womb. But the Bible thumpers do not care what the Bible teaches.

More importantly, if the Bible were followed, an abortion without the husband's permission would make the abortionist liable for an unlimited amount of damages – as determined by the husband and not any legal tribunal.

Biblically, the "Husband" and not the father. There is no scriptural prohibition related to an unwed woman terminating a fetus – to the contrary, sex out of wedlock is scorned and that makes fetus evidence of sin that should be disposed of.

If the fetus is suspected to be the result of infidelity, the woman is to be given an elixir that will induce a miscarriage or abortion {Numbers 5:11–31}. And, Deuteronomy 23:2 tells us: *"No one born of a forbidden union may enter the assembly of the Lord."* Moreover, that extends to their descendants for 250 years: *"Even to the tenth generation, none of his descendants may enter the assembly of the Lord."*

Pro-Life types don't go there. Their purpose is to harm people, not to follow the Bible. As pointed out in my 2012 book, *"Saint Paul's Joke,"* St. Paul established what could be seen as a New Testament trap – he warned that, if you take any part of the "law" you must take all of it. Cite scripture and you must be kosher, and your male children circumcised – only the male who is a recent convert is exempt from the circumcision.

Before the Civil War, the average Southern White Anglo-Saxon Protestant was a Democrat. At some point they became Republican. Their belief in political party doctrine being no less consistent than their Biblical one.

Consistent with Li'l Abner, they proudly violate Paul's mandate and the Climate Change affecting mandate in Leviticus 3:17: *"It Shall be a perpetual statute for your generations throughout all your dwellings, that ye eat neither fat nor blood."*

Medical science has affirmed the wisdom and necessity for following this law which is routinely violated in celebrations where pork is the main course. And that can of beans soaked in pork fat – the worst possible dietary fat – is a dietary staple of the underperformer.

Before you can target an audience, you must know that

audience. White Southern Evangelicals are those who promote their beliefs over facts – including the facts their beliefs are presumably based upon. Their lies and distortions of the truth to facilitate their goal of oppressing others are a characteristic they can identify with.

The lies must be told skillfully and contain a sufficient basis of truth to remain viable. Throughout its existence, the Republican Party has fielded candidates who present the truth in a form of lie that their base can accept. As the reader might already have realized, this mixture of fact and myth defines the foundation of Western religion.

From its 1828 origins among the supporters of Andrew Jackson and Martin Van Buren, the Democratic Party has been on the edge of the 4-Sister-Potus-Cousin structure. By its very nature, it has always been comfortable with both oppression and socialism. In many ways, it is the party of opportunists.

In case you haven't grasped the reality, slavery is a basic form of Socialism. The master serves as the state and provides food, clothing, lodging, and other common needs among the people. In exchange, the slaves do the work, while the master "governs."

Slavery is universal and timeless – we have no idea when the first slaves came into existence, and forms of slavery still exist. The failure to properly adjust the minimum wage is one example of using the system to, incrementally, impose slavery on the average person.

Liars will define slavery in terms of the deep south – the White master and Black slave. But Black slavery was Africans selling Africans – conquerors selling the conquered, rather than following the Exodus mandated slaughter of those who were conquered or perceived to be a threat to the "nation."

When your goal is personal power, when your audience is trained to accept lies, you lie to them. When you seek to improve the condition of your followers, you phrase the truth in terms of the myths they are accustomed to. This is what we see in the Hebrew Bible – fundamental truth shrouded in myth.

Strip away the myth, forget about any deity, look at the things that are mandated which can be phrased in scientific terms. Be the audience that the data is targeting.

The book starts with the importance of a diet governed by fruits and vegetables. Over time, the diet is modified and we learn to avoid milk and meat produced by the same animal – "do not cook a calf in its mother's milk."

The dating of the mandate comes at a time when early agriculture has been augmented by shepherds – sheep, goats, and cattle provide the protein once provided by hunters. Milk and cheese enter the human diet and reveal an allergy that does not seem to exist in those with Type-O blood {the common or original blood type of pre-modern humans}.

The Biblical era scholars are observing the changes and, without expressing the lactose intolerant concept in terms of the dual identical protein source, they realize the combination creates extreme diarrhea, gas, and bloating – and, in that era, possibly death.

They knew their audience; they knew that it would only take one person being sick after violating the rule, to bestow all the rules with an objectively affirmed "divine proof."

Do not consume blood – it carries pathogens that can be deadly. We are also told, as soon as possible, to wash any blood foreign from your clothes and body. They didn't need to know about germs, all they needed was to see the effect.

Your audience need not know why, they only need to see the effect. But, whatever you tell them must be in terms, have a context, they already accept.

Climate Chance has reinforced the wisdom of Leviticus 3:17 – *'This is a lasting ordinance for the generations to come, wherever you live: You must not eat any fat or any blood.'* The best way to avoid fat and blood is to avoid "red meat," and that reduces the effect "red meat" has as a contributing factor in global warming.

Because the presentation includes Bible references, an atheist might close their mind to science. If Atheists are your target demographic, then you have a problem – unless the goal is to inform them and ensure they will not comply.

If global warming were addressed through things like a change in diet, there would be no motivation to increase the use of wind and solar – or have the government initiate a program to install renewable generators on household rooftops.

Note, there are common characteristics defining policies supported or rejected by a specific demographic – one that does not mandate they reference or support something like the Bible. As a rule, people reject things that are personal and under their direct control, while advocating things that control the actions and freedoms of others.

We can judge and control individuals based on the "sins" they commit. We see often is the identification of "sin" as an act committed by others which is identified for the express purpose of controlling them.

Phrased properly, everything can become a sin; as with any hypnotist, the trick is to get the phrasing correct. You were born White, you're sin is racism and White Supremacy – that is the explanation for your position.

It doesn't matter that you are Jewish and the Holocaust claimed a thousand member of you known family, or that you overcame your profound dyslexia to achieve your status. Nor does it matter that your accuser came from a non-supportive family they are ashamed of.

Because of your skin color, you are the one responsible for their feelings toward their family and those they grew up with. Strangely, the White racist feels the same whenever they see a minority member doing better than they are. Neither side wants to take personal responsibility for their life.

Racist groups ignore the Golden rule, and the concept embodied in Matthew 7:1-2, *"The standard you use in judging is the standard by which you will be judged."* When we look at the post-2016 political environment see what happens when unfounded assertions by one side are turned against them.

In 2016, the Electoral College specifically functioned as designed. In the context of a Presidential Election, it functions like a Senate. But, Clinton Team yelled there had been Russian interference, some form of collusion, while AOC and others in Congress called for the elimination of the Electoral College.

Supposedly, Russia had successfully engaged in a level of vote manipulation and extensive election fraud in enough of the jurisdictions to manipulate the 2016 outcome. In 2020, there was a record voter turnout and, in one instance, viewers of the election coverage saw a massive vote switch occur within a two-minute reporting period. Again we had screams of "voter fraud" – this time from the Trump Camp. The "Big Lie" first birthed by Clinton was reborn with Trump.

With an appropriate change in phrasing, the same lie can serve both sides or divergent target audiences.

Ignorance occasionally allows the lie to work when the truth is there to contradict it.

When Evangelical bigots imposed *"Prohibition,"* they did so waving the Bile which boasted about Jesus turning water into wine – helping party-goers celebrate and get drunk. Since he wasn't a vineyard owner, Jesus was a mystical bootlegger – proponents of *"Prohibition"* would have imprisoned any Jesus who resurrected on 17 January 1920.

Imagine a Judgement Day when those who sponsored Prohibition, then followed it with the outlawing of marijuana, have to answer for that symbolically condemned the "water into wine." Would their judge be lenient enough to grant them eternal air-conditioning?

If your demographic are religious hypocrites, then your

linguistic technique would assist them in the performance of their sins. However, if like the Serpent, you are fulfilling some Devine Plan, would you will also warn them that their actions will lead to their eternal death?

Again, when we turn to Bible we are adhering to reality; in the United States, fully a third of the population claims to be *"true believers following the word of God"* – that they proudly violate at every opportunity.

When we toss aside ancient mythologies – things that existed long before what we call the dawn of civilization – we find a lot of what we now call science. As we see with the anti-vaxxers, science is also denied. And that denial occurs when the book they wave claims, in this era, a third of life shall die.

People like their superstitions; if they are related to or comprise your target demographic, you need to phrase things accordingly.

When dealing with the Pro-Life groups, you are dealing with those who support enormous expenditures for weapons of mass destruction and the insertion of American military might into nations around the world. You are dealing with those who support the mass murder of foreigners on foreign soil in what are undeclared wars – such as the twenty-year war started by President George W Bush.

Pro-life groups fail to promote healthcare for all – they help expedite death. They are in the business of killing and will kill whenever possible. They hold to one political party and set of semantics; they have counterparts in the other party engaged in the same behavior but are more circumspect.

Both sides seem to oppose the economically rational, and Bible-mandated universal healthcare. Both groups seem to enjoy the power they derived through the Covid-19 pandemic.

An interesting reality is how Biden seems to have quietly introduced the beginning of UBI in the form of a cash benefit to families with children.

Where do we find a modern Good Samaritan?

What phrasing will bring about the changes which will prepare the nation for the probable World war in 2033?

More important, what persuasive leader will emerge to prepare the nation for the Climate Change pandemics that the medical experts are envisioning?

What phrasing will resonate in a way that the naysayers are diminished in power?

Reality and facts vanish in their MSM and Social media presentations. Only the negative or downside comes through.

When the herd is stampeding, you cannot argue reality, you cannot stand in front of them and rationally explain why they should stop – if you do, you'll get crushed.

You need to run with them, get to the lead position, be acknowledged there; then, as leader of the stampede slowly turn them and bring them to a pasture where their need for food will calm them.

When they are fully at rest, peacefully grazing on green pasture, no challenger can take your leadership position. To do so requires they do so directly and in full view of a happy herd, content with its status.

If a challenger wants to take over the leadership, they must first scare the herd – create a threat to which the leader cannot respond.

Ideally, the threat is imaginary – but politically, it is a product of gossip and rumor. It is being told that the Emperor's New Clothes can only be seen by the wise and those ignorant enough to say they do not see the beautiful garments will be punished – or dismissed from the Royal Court.

Tell someone under hypnosis that the person in front of them is a criminal about to murder them or their loved ones, and tell them that, if they do something (e.g., push a button that kills the 'criminal' first) the threat would be eliminated – the self-defense phrasing will override other moral consideration and that person will commit an act they may otherwise believe to be cold-blooded murder.

As cited in Trump Card series Book 12, *"Life and Death in Satan's Swamp,"* Pelosi described her deception technique: *"'You smear somebody with falsehoods and all the rest, and then you merchandise it. [the reporters] write it, and then they say, 'See, it's reported in the press that this, this, this, and this.' So they have that validation that the press reported the smear, and then it's called the 'wrap-up smear.' And now I'm going to merchandise the press's report on the smear that we made. 'It's a tactic. And it's self-evident.'"*

Cite a third party and you are off the hook for the lie.

When President Ronald Reagan manipulated the data related to the Laffer Curve analysis of Great Britain's excessive taxation system, he promoted it as "Trickle Down Economics." It did not matter that American tax rates had been falling for over four decades and were well below the British equivalent. Nor did it matter that "Trickle Down Economics" went against all the economic development models that were proven to work.

The basic idea was, give the rich money, they will use it and the money used will trickle down and create the situation where *"a rising tide lifts all boats."* But the analogy requires that the water be poured into the area under the hulls of all the boats, not into the holds of the largest boats where it will either cause them to capsize or they will simply carry it out of port to sell somewhere else. As we know, when the money was spent, it was simply outsourced to nations with cheaper labor – thus China and India prospered, while the wealthy received profits that were exempt from American taxes.

We then heard calls to "Buy American" and get things that were "Made in the USA." But they didn't exist.

The Reagan administration saw a time when New Jersey decided to buy only American-made cars for the State fleet and discovered that only Volkswagen, a German Company, actually made its vehicles inside the USA. American automotive firms had outsourced their facilities to Canada and Mexico.

"American" firms maintained domestic corporate offices, but only so they could claim to still be "American," and because the executives didn't want to relocate. As a result, politicians redefined the term "Made in America" so the "Made in" became "substantially assembled in" – nothing needed "full" assembly, just the finishing touches of connected the pre-assemble parts.

Another instance of *"Change the name but everything remains the same."* That is how leaders do it – sometimes it is honest and a way to turn the stampeding herd; other times they are being dishonest and relying on the collective stupidity of the herd.

Anglo-Saxon traditions, like those defining the Roman adoption or invention of "Christianity," played the same word game. But it was also the game played with Noah's Flood.

As mentioned, Noah's Flood stated "sons of God" are the fathers of the men of renown – and all of them were erased by the flood. The flood was a popular legend that probably dated back to the end of the last glacial period; its use provided a familiar context for the declared transition in leadership

There was no flood, so the other religions never came to an end. However, it provided the foundation for claiming a new "divinely approved" religion. And, when it came time for the Romans to adopt and adapt Christianity, the first claim was that – like the previous men of renown – Jesus was genetically the child of the Hebrew deity and, as with the other men of renown, that he had a mortal mother, Mary.

What gave him importance over the other deities was the claim he was the direct heir of the deity and not its grandchild.

Now the Bible {Matthew 1:18-19} tells us that Mary and Joseph had been engaged, and when Mary returned from the visit with her family, she was pregnant; to save her from public disgrace, Joseph still married her.

The Church claims a "Holy Spirit" impregnated her, but it is more likely that King Herod was responsible – hence his desire to kill his only Jewish heir just as he had done with the sons by his Jewish Queen.

We are also told she went on to have other children. But all that was swept under the rug. Mary remains the perpetual virgin with Jesus as her only child.

As many academic theologians have done, a review of the Greek and Roman religions will show that, while names have been changed and legends consolidated, mythology remained the same. The Bible says Jesus was born in the spring – when the shepherds were in the fields – but the Roman Church chose the popular Winter Solstice holiday of Saturnalia for the birth date.

They knew their audience and knew doctrines of social equality were becoming popular with the masses and Hebrew teachings were based on equality and an end of, or escape from, "slavery" of the type which marked Roman society. Eventually, Europeans would paint Africans as the descendants of Ham so they could impose Genesis 9:25, *"Cursed be Canaan* [the son of Ham]; *a servant of servants shall he be unto his brethren,"* to justify black slaves.

It's commonly recognized that Saturnalia traditions – merrymaking, gift-giving, the lighting of candles, feasting, and singing – still define the holiday. Only the names and supposed symbolism or reason for the activity changed – and, as pagan nations were conquered and "converted," new elements were added.

The ancient reverence for trees that gave us the "Tree of Knowledge" had a different form among the Germanic tribes; when Britain's Queen Victoria married Prince Albert, he introduced the German tree to the British Empire and America.

Victoria married Albert on 10 February 1840, the Irish potato famine began in 1845, and the immigration to America began the following year. And while Germans had been arriving since the 1600s, the Industrial Revolution saw the start of a major migration which increased sharply with the failed social revolutions of 1848 – the era of The Communist Manifesto that defined the social theories of Marx and Engels.

In the 1880s, German Chancellor Otto von Bismarck rephrased the doctrines to create old-age pensions that – since FDR – we now recognize as Social Security Insurance. Again, we can recognize it as a rephrasing of Marx, in the context of rephrasing of the Old and New Testaments. But some want to wave the Bible and complain about its teachings – while also yelling people should follow those teachings.

When you understand who your audience is, you find the basis for phrasing things in a manner that convinces them to form a circular firing squad – to attack the very positions they traditionally advocate. In some cases, you usurp the position by adopting or subverting a core tenet of the opposing position.

We saw an example with the Biblical "men of renown" who were the half-mortal children of the sons of a primal deity – all of whom "died in the flood." However, since there was no flood, those pagan beliefs continued and expanded – in terms of the Biblical timeline, we can say they were "re-instituted" as the basis for the various pantheons associated with the Greek, Roman, Egyptian, and Viking Deities.

Seventeen hundred years ago, Constantine the Great saw Christianity as a way to unify and control his empire, so he was quick to accept the idea that Jesus was "the only begotten son" of the primary deity – a starting point ancient Egyptians called the "self-begotten beginning," and modern science just accepts as the explanation of how the physical universe appeared from absolute nothing. Atheists avoid what science accepts: the universe is eternal and meets one of the definitions of "God."

When von Bismarck introduced old-age pensions, he was undermining the 48'er movement that had emerged from, and as part of, the same economic theories set forth by Karl Marx in

1843. A century later America has McCarthyism, and the focus is placed on Marx being anti-religion – McCarthy's base was the anti-Semitic Evangelical Protestant who, in Germany, had also backed Hitler.

Published in 1848, *The Communist Manifesto* provided the basis for the attacks by stating: *"Communism abolishes eternal truths, it abolishes all religion, and all morality, instead of constituting them on a new basis; it, therefore, acts in contradiction to all past historical experience."*

An eternal truth is that whatever went before is wrong. Thus we have the "Cancel Culture" that wishes to erase history because it existed in a context that they do not accept. This is a prelude to confrontation, and confrontation is what their base wants – revolution being the ultimate goal.

As Marx warned: *"Keep people from their history and they are easily controlled."* He's also quoted as expressing this with the words: *"If you can cut people off from their history, then they can easily be persuaded."*

A primary goal of those supporting the "Cancel Culture" is to persuade, control, and subjugate the masses.

A true leader does not want confrontation. The Stallion that moves into the leadership position will not confront a herd that must be scared and is therefore running mindlessly toward its own destruction. A lead stallion, a true leader, will simply assume the leadership role and from there turns the herd.

You cannot turn the mindless mob by confronting it – it will run over you and crush them. But those who cause the stampede, those who promote fear, want that revolutionary crushing to occur – they promote fear.

It is only when the herd is at peace and quietly grazing that those seeking to assume leadership will seek confrontation. The herd is at peace and most will not notice that their leader has been changed – nor will they care.

As a leader, you must know your audience. You must

also recognize that leadership takes many forms. The Goal can be altruistic, egotistic, or purely based on immediate personal gain. However, genetically, leaders often just emerge as needed and from a common family line or ancestry.

If we stay with the herd analogy, all leadership provides status. For the average herd animal, being the leader means having a choice of mates and the ability to procreate so that their genes eventually dominate the herd. If those genes are superior – as is normally the case – the quality of the herd will improve and eventually assume leadership over other herds. As time goes on, so long as the general population increases, the species improves. If a flaw enters the genetic pool, or the herd becomes too genetically similar to the point of effectively being clones – the species can no longer improve, so it dies.

When dealing with humans, we speak of races or tribes within a race. Again, we can turn to the animal husbandry that was used to create the Biblical marriage laws – the twelve tribes are the pool of genetic variation, and the thirteenth, the Levites and Kohanim, are the leadership. The leaders will emerge from the general population of a tribe, marry into the Levites who rule the tribe, and their children will then have a right to marry across the tribal borders into the Levites of other tribes, or into the ruling Levites.

If we invent other ways to identify tribes, we see those rules hold – these are the relationships in "Jonathon's POTUS COUSINS" and when talking of descendants of Charlemagne or the 4-Sisters. Curiously, a leader is not always the one who formally "takes the lead." Quite often, they emerge only when the circumstances force them into a leadership role. Altruism is the driving force and they will do things so that the credit or notoriety goes to someone else.

When the driving force is greed or short-term profit, the alleged leader will stimulate fear; they become the reason that the herd will stampede; they are the ones who dishonestly yell fire in a crowded theater; they are the ones behind malware and other cyber attacks.

They are not leaders. They are criminals – though not always seen as such. One example was set by William Randolph Hearst and is being followed by many in the modern media and its distorted reporting of alleged "facts" that serve to promote social discord and discontent.

As we know from the popularity of a "house of horrors," the amusement park steeplechase, and horror movies, fear has a solid market; the general public loves their adrenaline high. The problem comes when stress levels trigger a stampede.

Fear is a factor in the Covid-19 Pandemic being used to reshape the economic landscape into the one envisioned by the 48'ers when their 1847/8 European rebellion failed and gave rise to the changes that led to the American Civil War and the introduction of von Bismarck's German Socialist programs.

With words of German-Jewish Karl Marx, augmented by other intellectuals of his era, Biblical Socialism was launched. However, Marx expressed a curious reality that can only be understood by leaders and became a defining force among the group whose audience or base is derived from the Evangelicals: *"Communism begins where Atheism begins."*

As I have noted, the basic premise or definition of "God" is that of the beginning of all things the "nothing" which gave birth to the universe, where both "God" and the "Universe" are "eternal."

As we saw, the famous recipe shows us how mass can be converted into energy or decelerated energy can become mass. But reality dictates there is no way to eliminate either mass or energy. All things, all physical matter (or mass) is composed of energy. Thus, without energy, there is no physical existence.

By definition "God" is the "Universe" or the purest form of energy. When Marx referred to Atheism he was referring to those inclined to dismiss the remnants of pagan mythology that form a basis for Christianity. Dismiss God, you are dismissing existence or one linguistic term for the origin of existence.

Marx focused on the idea that: *"The democratic concept of man is false, because it is Christian. The democratic concept holds that ... each man is a sovereign being. This is the illusion, dream, and postulate of Christianity."* Thus we can infer that he was equating Atheism with a rejection of Christianity and all the lies and hypocrisy that comprise its basic ritual structure.

The audience Marx was targeting was fed-up with being ruled by the Christian Church and those concepts which were consistently hypocritical and promoted for the sole purpose of repression.

There is a proverb that seems to have emerged in 1885, in a book by novelist Anne Isabella Thackeray Ritchie: *"If you give a man a fish, he eats for a day; If you teach a man to fish, he eats for a lifetime."* Variations on this proverb date back millennia and, being timeless, its true origins are irrelevant.

The 12th-century philosopher Maimonides spoke against charity and in favor of teaching a trade. The idea is that people should *"earn an honest livelihood and not be forced to the dreadful alternative of holding up [their] hand for charity."*

Marx, who died in 1883, is quoted saying: *"Catch a man a fish, and you can sell it to him. Teach a man to fish, and you ruin a wonderful business opportunity."* In a variation on this thought, he is also quoted saying: *"Capitalism: Teach a man to fish, but the fish he catches aren't his. They belong to the person paying him to fish, and if he's lucky, he might get paid enough to buy a few fish for himself."*

It has humor and can be used to explain the idea behind monopoly practices and the root benefit of slavery – to the slave owner. But the second quote is more interesting.

When Henry Ford was building his automotive business, he reportedly paid workers an above-market wage – he wanted to ensure they had enough income to afford the cars they built, which was a form of "advertising" derived from more cars being seen, and that resulted in more cars being sold.

When DNA testing was being promoted for genealogy, and researchers wanted to build a database, the tests were free – now there is a thriving business with tests costing over $100 each. That's more than 15 hours of minimum wage labor to find out the origins and history of your genetic structure; having that knowledge could warn you that you are at risk for any number of inherited diseases.

If everyone had a poverty-level income – referred to as a Universal Basic Income {UBI} – the number of basic goods and services sold would increase; that would increase the funds that would buy the next level of goods or services, and the economy would grow.

Granted, there would be some who did not work – but that only means they would not have additional money, or they would devote their time to the arts, sciences, and other honest endeavors which offer a future benefit. It also means that there would be no need for charity or welfare – an enormous savings in government cost – while economic growth would generate more tax revenues.

Economically, for society as a whole, all technological and cultural gain can be linked to a skill being widely practiced among a population striving to enhance production efficiency.

But you need to know your audience, or capture and trap them. And, for now, in 2021, we still have an audience that is opposed to anything that might improve economic efficiency.

It becomes a game of semantics. From the 1980s Reagan and into the Bush Jr. era, we had an attack on Social Security. If we said we could not afford it, or that the fund was being depleted because inflation had brought incomes over the cap level – this meant the excess was excluded from supporting the system, so the inflation-adjusted payments were not offset by an inflation-adjusted income contributing to the system. This meant that the wealthy profited through an effective tax reduction. The record shows, they then received an additional tax reduction based on changes in deductions and overall tax rates.

The government lost "surplus capital" it was dependant upon to balance the budget. People were forced into poverty and the Welfare programs kicked in – further damaging federal and state budgets.

Marx believed in using "surplus capital" to improve the lot of those on the bottom. The "surplus capital" would be used to improve the health of, and teach skills to, those who would otherwise be dependent upon charity – a single-parent mother who has been denied an abortion and is forced to have a child because she was raped, the condom broke, or her diaphragm shifted.

Maybe the person was harmed by bigotry and racism. It doesn't matter. Society is predicated on inequality at all levels. Even the expression "Black Lives Matter" is another way of declaring that Asian and European lives are meaningless – a reality that will be recognized when the minority becomes the majority.

Predicted by birthrates and the open border policies that Reagan promoted and Biden reintroduced, we know where the demographics are headed. Americans knowingly voted for the reversal – their desire for open borders was behind objections to Trump's "Wall" – which was only a structural improvement of the Secure Fence Senator Obama legislated in 2006 and, a few years later, built as POTUS.

Biden's policy, which he deemed important enough to introduce early in his first hundred days, showed that, as Vice President, he secretly opposed his boss' border immigration policies. At the end of the first 100-days, the media reported that Biden had a 63% approval rating – so the people approve of the open borders and the welfare costs that come with them.

It is, after all, democratic – the result that they voted for.

As Marx phrased it: *"The oppressed are allowed once every few years to decide which particular representatives of the oppressing class are to represent and repress them."*

If Biden once supported Obama, but now has obviously rejected the 2006 Secure Fence Act, it infers there was a change in the target audience. Biden knows his audience; having been in the business of kowtowing to the mass mentality since 1972, he has proven he is a master at following the herd.

It took 49-years for Biden to gain a lead stallion position – by defeating a man who had required only a year to obtain the same position. But, where Trump angered the herd by leading, Biden follows from the front and it raises the question: What is the demographic description of the group they want to capture?

Is the herd stampeding, grazing, or in transition between the two?

It is a hard question. But not as hard as one that seeks to discern if the stallion is a leader or a follower.

Is he a Joseph R. Biden, avoiding press conferences and minimizing opportunities to be attacked? Or Donald J. Trump, a person who makes their presence felt and, even when out of office, remains in control as a force to be reckoned with?

Who are you to yourself and those closest to you?

If you know that then you are a step closer to deciding on your target demographic – the audience that will most likely commit to your product. And when you know your audience, you know what will resonate with them – you also know what you need to get your instincts into that same mental mode. In effect, you come off as "one of them" – they feel comfortable with you and with the instruction you provide.

Since you belong to their group– you can be trusted.

Comically, when your target demographic believes you belong, any attack on you becomes an attack on them. Your enemies are their enemies; disparaging your trustworthiness infers that they are not to be trusted. The attacks serve to make your base stronger – carbon turning iron into tempered steel.

The weakest position is that derived from a blind dislike for "the other." The stampeding herd runs from that which they fear; eventually, they will stop to graze and they need a leader they feel will protect them. Depending on leadership qualities, and the rationality of its goals or policies, the stallion becomes stronger or weaker.

Since it only takes a minor flaw or weakness, on the part of the aggressor, for the attack to fail, Trump welcomes attacks.

If the core policies are sound, when the attacks end, the policies will still be there and will have proved to be viable – the stature of the proponents will be increased. History will forget or denigrate those whose policies are illogical.

Socialism and the support of scholars date to a period that predates the Exodus. Biden expressed support for both.

In 1776, the Founding Fathers declared a separation of Church and State. Karl Marx was born in 1818 and declared the "Church" to be a source of socioeconomic problems. Between 1945 and 2021, American Church attendance fell by 50%.

A good leader attacks the core beliefs of the opposition; at first, this triggers a backfire effect and events that cause the opposing forces to self-destruct; then the leader steps in. In the era of Covid-19, Marxist policies became temporary "stimulus packages" – when they become permanent, there will be record economic growth.

The historic "Problem" is resolved.

The only leadership issue is one predicated on the intent of the leader. Are they out for personal power, or to better the lives of the herd?

At this time of historic transitions and environmental changes that will last a century, who is their target audience?

CHAPTER Five - Defining Changes

There is an overriding characteristic of those opposed to change, they take issue with new technology, science, medicine, or anything that disrupts their dogmatic approach to life.

As a rule, these Luddites oppose those things which will benefit them while they are being negatively affected by things other than the one they are opposing.

Change is necessary and comes about slowly. More often than not, it's the unopposed things, things with not objectively logical basis, that are or will eventually do the most harm.

Instead of acknowledging the past, Luddites often argue to keep the social norms through the erasure of the memory of that harm. In "The Life of Reason," the pragmatist philosopher George Santayana stated: *"Those who cannot remember the past are condemned to repeat it."*

We generally know the quote – be it directly or via some paraphrasing such as that of Sir Winston Churchill: *"Those who fail to learn from history are doomed to repeat it."*

Roughly 170 pages of text provide the foundation for the Churchill version, and they are prefaced by: *"Progress, far from consisting in change, depends on retentiveness. When change is absolute there remains no being to improve and no direction is set for possible improvement: and when experience is not retained, as among savages, infancy is perpetual."*

Think about this. Progress does not consist of change, it is dependent upon retentiveness. If we do not retain the lessons and experiences of the past, and those know what progress has carried us beyond, we will fall back on and repeat the errors of the past.

The Cancel Culture movement wants to ensure we forget the history when they should be correcting it – providing the context that brought about the events. American slavery was not true slavery, it was just how it appeared in the New World.

It has always existed in some form, in the modern industrial world it is "wage slavery."

Members of the "Cancel Culture" want to erase the role global slavery played in American evolution. They want to erase the reality that slavery can take many forms and that religious slavery was a driving force behind emigration. When we look at the process of creating the Constitution, we see the economic and taxation issues expressed as "free" or "slave" – wage labor or generationally indentured – economic structures.

Indentured servitude was a personal debt-driven "wage slavery." The slavery that brought Africans to the New World was driven by dominant African or Muslim tribes profiting off their captives. The model for that behavior can be seen in the Roman conquest of Europe, among the Greeks, Egyptians, and back through all the dominant cultures.

In the modern world, it takes the form of militaristic or economic dominance which forces people in third world nations to work in sweatshop conditions for poverty wages to produce we casually use and then discard. But, because they are halfway around the world, it is a nebulous form of slavery.

In America, slavery provided agricultural labor for cash crops like cotton and tobacco that were critical for international trade. Transporting those crops provided a "Tall Ship" industry that took advantage of New England forests. In combination, they gave rise to the "Triangle Trade" – one leg of which was the transportation of African slaves, who would still have been held in slavery, only they would have been living in worse conditions and with life expectancies shortened by tropical diseases which claimed the lives of vast numbers of "Triangle Trade" sailors.

Indirectly, shipping provided a basis for the evolution of the Ivy League University system.

The foundation for Harvard University was laid while the Plymouth colonialists were still settling in. But it was ships and the "Triangle Trade" which funded university expansion so vital to the mercantile culture – an ancient reality represented in the co-dependent Bible tribes: Zebulun {merchants] and Issachar {scholars}.

The Cancel Culture wishes to suppress the history that should be celebrated – but not repeated. Instead, they want to destroy the monuments marking the points of change that have brought us to this point in our history, and they want to teach Critical Race Theory. In a melting pot nation where interracial, interreligious, cross-ethnic marriages are a regular event, they want to teach young children that skin color is more important than their intellect or work ethic.

Those who attack history attack change and they should consider where they would be if it had not occurred.

All Americans arrived here from somewhere else – even "Native" Americans have their ancestral roots in Asia. North American tribal groups have European and African DNA mixed in with their genetic Asian origin base.

America is a "mixing pot," a smelting furnace creating a new race of humans – the Cancel Culture is just one example of slag rising and becoming visible at the top. But the beauty of leadership is that, eventually, a leader appears who skims away the slag and forms the remaining alloy into a thing of beauty.

Those who do not like having been forced to become part of the process are free to reserve tickets on a plane headed to their ancestral region of origin. Those who wish to continue to complain about the past, can track down the branch of their family still in the place of origin – and know for certain, if not for that immigrant ancestor, they would have been better off.

Of course, if not for the immigrant ancestor, they would not exist at all. The true basis for their demonstrations is self-loathing. But, forget about those mindless self-hating bigots who exist only because of the American past they seek to cancel.

They are only capable of expressing hatred, negativity, and voicing complaints about society – their existence is that of slag floating to the surface.

If not for slavery, the American merchant fleet might not have emerged to dominate global trade routes; nor could it have retained that role until the emergence of the steel ships – with their roots in the 1860 ironclad ships. While their design and construction were not initiated in the United States, their first use in battle was in the Civil War when, on 12 October 1861, the CSS Manassas confronted a Union ship at the Battle of the Head of Passes.

The Civil War initiated a new age in American evolution – it spawned the development of the Rust Belt region and was fed by the education promoted by mercantile Northern States.

Initially, the Colonialists sent their children to England for an education. However, New England's prosperity is linked to Harvard (founded in 1635/6), which was the seed from which emerged other Ivy League Colleges: Yale, Princeton, Columbia, University of Pennsylvania, Brown, and Dartmouth.

Merchants and Education were in the North. The upper crust of Virginia continued to send their children to England – they didn't see the wisdom of supporting education.

As time progressed, Southerners passed laws forbidding education – this validated the existence of a lower-class white *'Hillbilly'* culture and *'Lil Abner'* stereotype of the pork eating ignoramus partnered with sexy dumb females. Since slaves were to be denied even the most basic education, it became ingrained their mentality and culture; the northern migration transplanted the Southern to Northern minority communities.

The Southerners, learning nothing from the Bible they love to wave about, created what Santayana saw as *"barbarians, in whom instinct has learned nothing from experience."*

Prior to 1900, Confederate States *"Southern Yellow Dog Democrats"* – individuals who, without thinking, would vote for a "Yellow Dog," if it identified as a Democrat. That ingrained bias also a part of the northern cultural migration and persisted to the point that Biden could assert: *"If you have a problem figuring out whether you're for me or Trump, then you ain't black."*

If only instinctively, Biden understands that members of the Black community have yet to shed the thinking and training which defined their great grandparents. Biden acknowledged that "the Sins of the fathers" can be passed down through three or generations – they last over a century.

The Northern States, which had received the influx of the European 48ers were the Republican "Progressives" – Socialists who were following an ideology based on economic theories that said we should lift the lower classes above poverty. It was the idea of being the "Good Samaritan" under conditions where aid to the poor was derived from the "surplus capital" generated by the successful.

Today we interlink Progressive with Socialist, with Marx and Communist – in principle, the underlying economics is the same Zebulun-Issachar synergy that allowed Hebrew culture its ongoing place in history and that allowed the Northern Colonies to emerge as the American economic core for a growing nation; as the nation expanded we see that economic power is matched to the locations with prestigious universities.

In April 2021, President Joe Biden praised the education system and credited it a century of American economic growth. He then acknowledged we were in a period of transition, that times had changed and the educational system of the past was insufficient to provide a foundation for future prosperity.

Biden introduced two realities – one I have addressed in previous books with the reference to a quote attributed to Saint Ignatius of Loyola by Voltaire: *"Give me the child for the first seven years and I will give you the man."* The other is that we need to go beyond High School if we are to keep pace with the technology that will give rise to Artificial Intelligence as a part of our daily lives.

We now know that children begin to learn while still in the womb and that they are actually shaped by the frequencies existing while their brains are developing in the womb – this starts about six weeks after fertilization and defines a period in which significant aspects of infant personality are created.

It has been established that playing music to the fetus – and talking to it – will contribute to a child that emerges after a period of nine or ten months. We normally say nine months or 266 days from the moment of conception; the ancient Greeks said the period was ten 30-day months; because I know when fertilization occurred, I can state my six children were 305-days from fertilization – that period same period seems consistent with my maternal siblings (I lack data for my paternal ones).

The key element for this divergence is that the adult is being created from week seven and that creation is tied to the frequencies it is exposed to – which also explains the observed basis that gave rise to birth month astrology.

In ancient times, when astrology first can into existence, an average person spent their whole life within a 25-mile radius of where they were born. Seismic and other vibrational factors were consistent and associated with various times of the year – controlled by weather, daylight hours, and related activities or celebrations (music, etc).

We can go so far as to say that seasonal conditions also controlled when children were born – New York experienced a surge in births, nine months after the 9 November 1965 New York City or Great Northeast Blackout.

In an interview, Dr. Bruce H. Lipton once explained that from birth to age seven, theta waves control our world. These are waves of a lower vibrational frequency than your conscious mind can perceive, but are a catalyst for childhood imagination and sculpting the subconscious.

Oh, for those who are wondering, Bruce is two weeks younger than me, and was born 35 miles from my birth location

– since I'm adopted there is no direct relationship. But I do like his perspective. In the case of Covid-19, he points out what I have already published – it is the underlying, pre-existing, issue that makes Covid-19 deadly.

The virus itself does not kill, but it is the fact the body is already fighting medical problems that kill. He has also pointed out that, in terms of health, *"Do not put the fear in your head, because the function of the mind is to manifest whatever you believe."* MSM and politicians understand this, so, to control you, they push the fear.

As he points out, by pushing the idea of lockdowns and isolation, they also create the basis for a second, third, and fourth "spike."

This is because by isolating people they are not exposed and therefore their immune systems cannot adjust for the virus. At the same time, the isolation increases the stress and fear that compromises the immune system – ensuring that any exposure will serious enough to make people sick and the stress aids pre-existing conditions to get worse. When the two come together, people die. And the fearmongers get new ammunition.

As I emphasized in the Trump Card series, Covid-19 is a culling virus. Any culling virus can trigger other self-induced medical conditions and so we see that the CDC weekly numbers reveal a small increase in "Deaths From All Causes" while we hear of the enormous number {about the same as deaths from cigarette smoke} of Covid related deaths, while the other areas of routine fatality fall and are ultimately reduced to the point where the relative numbers are sharply negative.

So, going back to education, what we place in the child's mind after the first trimester then, after birth, add to during the next seven years of existence, yields the adult.

One thing that was learned is that rhythmic music – the type associated with many classical pieces or meditation – will serve to calm the fetus and the resulting infant will suffer less stress. You'll have a more peaceful child that wants to learn – allowing for other inherited factors, their IQ will be higher.

Carrying this logic forward, we see common elements in "Minority Communities" where the music is not something that relaxes – you would play it when you are going to sleep.

There is also, because "mediation music" is important, a question of the House of Worship a family might attend – that a pregnant woman might regularly attend. All too often, a fetus goes through their gestation dominated by the rousing rhythms which internalize a level of persistent rhythmic stress which then defines their life.

Consider the difference between two pregnant women – one regularly attends a vibrant African-American Church and the other an orthodox synagogue. The first has exciting shout-out music, the other has a form of prayer that involves davening – a whole body rhythmic rocking during prayer, where the pace roughly matches a pace of a resting heartbeat. The former will enhance stress levels, the latter lowers them, and that rhythmic difference is hard-wired into the resulting baby.

If we take that child, introduce them to a pre-school that promotes calm learning, their emotional rhythm will be altered or enhanced; if that is reinforced at home, the child becomes productive.

Of course, upper social classes will promote pre-school – their children have been wired for lower internal stress and, therefore, are ready to learn – they accept the stress that comes with learning new skills or ways to see the world.

We define change as both the way we change ourselves and how we change the world around us. Those programmed for stress will immediately turn to violence as their means of affecting change. Those programmed for calm will quietly act to change things – and if the change does not happen, they can wait for events to alter the environment and make the change possible.

In May 2021, the media reported genetic researchers had determined humans could live between 120 and 150 years. It is just a matter of emotional or psychological stress.

As one researcher was quoted saying: "*Aging in humans exhibits universal features common to complex systems operating on the brink of disintegration. This work is a demonstration of how concepts borrowed from physical sciences can be used in biology to probe different aspects of senescence and frailty to produce strong interventions against aging.*"

The human lifespan exhibits a direct correlation between aging and the ability to cope with stress. As stated by the study author, Timothy V. Pyrkov, "*As we age, more and more time is required to recover after a perturbation, and on average we spend less and less time close to the optimal physiological state.*"

It appears there is consistency between the physical and biological sciences when discussing stress that revolves around resiliency. Healthy humans are very resilient; loss of resilience is directly related to chronic diseases and elevated levels of all-cause mortality risks. The Covid pandemic demonstrated how a minor stressor virus, when introduced into individuals under severe stress from other medical issues, becomes fatal – hence it is a culling virus.

Research is showing that two parameters that control life expectancy: physiological and chronological age. In terms we can all understand, consider two cars that are of the same design and model year, one that has extensive "wear and tear" while the other is "pristine". Which one is likely to give the best performance and command the better used-car market price?

Our society is comprised of cultural segments devoted to the adding of "wear and tear." The approach to Covid-19 has shown one example of that devotion and how it contributed to increased violence and drug use. In California, whose media and political leaders promoted both forms of stress inducement, the number of drug overdoses doubled.

In December 2020, San Francisco's city taxpayer-funded Drug Overdose Prevention and Education Project reported that 621 people died of drug overdoses – roughly five times more than the 173 deaths related to the coronavirus during the same period. And keep in mind, the coronavirus deaths were among those whose existing medical conditions meant they were likely to die within six months – or remain alive in a vegetative state.

Looking to the science and the effect of stress, we can add to the stress of some by, once again, citing from the Bible – Psalm 90:10 describes a modern life expectancy, *"The years of our life are seventy, or even by reason of strength eighty; yet their span is but toil and trouble; they are soon gone, and we fly away."*

In Genesis 6:3, we see an earlier statement that agrees with both the science and observed reality: *"My Spirit shall not abide in man forever, for he is flesh: his days shall be 120 years."*

In reality, we have a woman who lived in Arles, France, Jeanne Louise Calment, whose fully document life of 122 years and 164 days (21 February 1875 – 4 August 1997) has placed her annals of history as a fully documented example of the scientific projection, the Genesis assertion, and years attributed to Moses and Aaron.

Could life expectancy be a direct result of stress? And is it possible that, during gestation, we teach our children to die by imposing unnecessary stress upon them – by not teaching their brains to maintain a calm rhythm?

Having programmed humanity for stress, ignorance, and early death, the Mainstream Media {MSM} then assumes the reigns – honoring the mantra command, "if it bleeds it leads" – and continues to impose stress with its focus on any negative event, perspective, or "spin" they can assert to increase stress levels and cause social unrest.

If we use Israel as an example of induced stress, we see Hamas leaders would rather kill Israelis than guide their people to prosperity through peace. And in the USA, "leaders" like 'he Squad actively cheer the self-destructive Hamas approach and blame Israel for defending itself and taking responsive actions to protect its people.

The traditional stress-inducing anti-Semites ignore or chose to forget that Israel was the original Hebrew homeland – until Rome expelled them – and ignore the fact descendants of those Romans continued the persecution until it culminated in the Holocaust. They ignore the fact that before the Holocaust Hitler tried to expel Jews from Germany, but the rest of Europe would not accept them – nor would the United States, which had already created anti-Jewish immigration laws limiting the immigration from Hebrew dominated Eastern Europe. Modern Israel exists because of European anti-Semitism that is now the basis for those who support Hamas and will eventually cause a Third World War (sometime around 2033).

In 2020, Covid-19 triggered "stimulus packages" that are just basic income and medical care programs of the type that Progressives have called for since 1843. These programs are designed to alleviate stress among the foundational classes of society, while also supporting the economy in a way that will make existing upper classes prosper and grow numerically.

However, since the goal is to induce stress, we are seeing those who promote fear helping the process by promoting the intellectually infamous Cloward-Piven Strategy.

Cloward-Piven Strategy was a 1966 "Hippy Era" political strategy that called for the overloading of the welfare system so it will collapse and be replaced by a more efficient system – in some ways we could say they wanted the type of economy that existed in the "Star Trek" universe that appeared on TV screens in the same year.

As Trekkies know, the Star Trek Universe is a cashless society in which basic needs can be met using replicators that recycle waste products by restructuring atoms. Obviously, the fictional universe contains many things we can relate to – but they are presented as cultural elements of alien societies.

In the real world, we are moving to a cashless society in which deposits are made directly to a bank account, charges are placed on a credit or debit card and payment is drawn from that bank account. Stimulus packages establish the government can easily direct welfare payments to consumer bank accounts. But as economics indicates, we don't need welfare – we need basic, above the poverty level, automatic income going to everyone who is an adult citizen and holds a valid Social Security number.

As of July 2021, Biden's Administration began delivering money in the form of monthly Child-Credit cash payments. The system delivers half the credit monthly and the other half when the recipient does their annual tax filing.

The immediate effects would be a total elimination of welfare with all its related government personnel or operating expenses and, in terms of personal Income Taxes, elimination of both personal and itemized deductions. Taxes would only apply to earned income – the Universal Basic Income would be fully exempt from the numeric process.

Corporate taxes, capital gains, or business income would be the only taxable income – and those taxes would actually be lower. {I know, sounds weird and counterintuitive, but that is what the math dictates.} And the rate could be fixed – no need for a graduated income tax and, therefore, fewer chances of the wealthy corporations paying nothing.

Either the corporation made a cash profit or they did not – if they made a profit they pay the fixed rate; if they make no profit they either brake-even on costs or will go out of business. For individuals: they had income, so they pay taxes.

Some could say – as was asserted in the context of the stimulus unemployment payment supplement and extension – that people would not work. But the logic behind that assertion is based on the assumption that people prefer living in poverty over living a secure and productive life.

Granted, UBI would mean workers would avoid survival jobs and chose emotionally satisfying employment or they can seek intellectually stimulating employment. But, the average person will work – in a two-adult household, there would be two UBI deposits, and, therefore, one could afford to stay home and care for the kids.

Among healthy seniors on Social security, we see some working and others enjoying their retirement. It's a matter of personal choice and in both cases, the economy still benefits.

But the idea is to keep creating new crises while making the government so big that the entire system collapses.

This is not just a Cloward-Piven Strategy application, it is a driving force behind many governmental policies. Elected officials are focused on today and the next election. They do not care about what happens after they leave the office or are dead.

If we look back at Reaganomics, the economic approach treated debt is meaningless. The underlying assumption was that at some point before the debt would be paid, there would be a level of inflation so high that the value of the fixed dollar-denominated debt owed would shrink to nothing.

To understand, consider the cost of gasolene in 1966 – you could buy three gallons for a dollar, about thirty cents – in 2021, under Biden, the pump price is around $3.09. Imagine you borrowed a thousand dollars in 1966 and used the money to buy some silver at $1.30/ounce – in mid-2021, it was $27.50. Your $1,000 investment is equal to $21,000 and you can pay the loan by selling 37 of the 769 ounces you originally bought.

Reaganomics assumed any benefits derived increase in value while the value of the debt decreased. If you can trigger inflation quickly enough, the interest on the debt is also erased – but you still have the purchased asset.

Of course, we screw ourselves when we seek to have low

inflation and continue increasing the debt. But that only means that, when we do get inflation, it will be record-setting.

In an ideal world, paychecks and the contents of savings accounts would, by law, be adjusted for inflation – whenever the inflation rate exceeds 10%. If that were done, the economy would benefit from inflation. I'll leave you to figure out why, but consider that all debt would vanish while the average person would retain their purchasing power. Of course, there is no need to adjust the stock market – stocks self-adjust and so ensure the wealthy investor retain their wealth.

As individuals, we define the changes we want to see. It is well known that many people are opposed to change and they are generally called "Conservative" because, whether or not it is beneficial to the continuity and advancement of the species, they chose to conserve what is.

At the beginning of the modern age, at the beginning of the Industrial Revolution in Britain, as weaving factories were mechanized, those who stood in opposition came to be known as Luddites – their emergence corresponded to the final of the American Revolution and extended into the time period marked by the War of 1812.

Today they would be identified as suffering from some form of "technophobia" or "technophobic." And while there are similarities, it is not the same as being an anti-vaxxer.

When properly applied, the term "Progressive" refers to those who are in favor of progress and promoted various forms of reasoned change. A "Progressive' might hold that there is no rational reason for someone to spend long hours at work simply for the sake of working – the only economically import element is productivity. It is not how many acres of land are devoted to farming, rather it is the quality and quantity of crops that are produced on each acre.

When proposed, the state purpose of the Cloward-Piven Strategy was described in a May 1966 article, "The Weight of the Poor: A Strategy to End Poverty" which stated that, "*The ultimate objective of this strategy – to wipe out poverty by establishing a guaranteed annual income – will be questioned by some. Because the ideal of individual social and economic mobility has deep roots, even activists seem reluctant to call for national programs to eliminate poverty by the outright redistribution of income.*"

The concept failed because it used the semantic idea that it involved an "*outright redistribution of income.*" As we have seen many times since the Great Depression, it is not an income redistribution, it is an economic stimulus based on the creation of a solid economic foundation that eliminates the need for social welfare programs now proven to be government subsidies of below poverty wages. That is, welfare for rich slave "owners."

The economy would be far more sustainable if people did not "need" to work, but worked to enhance their standard basic of living. For employers, the goal would not be to have warm bodies running around, but rather to enhance productivity – in that way lower the body count so the total wages paid remained the same but each employee was paid more while profits grew.

Most of economics discussed here as changes which must be made for the United States to remain viable are thins which exist in other nations.

We hear the "Socialism" rant applied to dictatorships that are little more than classic feudal monarchies.

Real socialism can be viewed as either Biblical or Viking – in many ways it is both, with Capitalism as the cherry on top.

Because of the combined effects of Global Warming and the Internet, in terms of sedentary ethnic-tribal cultures, the world is about to end.

Global Warming will drive all those in equatorial regions north – bringing with them various tropical diseases. As that happens, regional populations at or above the latitude of Spain will increase significantly.

Modern leaders will be defined and remembered by their ability to prepare their nations for the changes which will occur between 2025 and 2050.

During this period, many classic religions will experience significant changes. In this discussion, the focus must remain on the Abrahamic religions that define the Middle Eastern and Western cultures. We can dismiss religious influence in China – either their system of government will expand the traditional folk religions and Confucianism, or it will be dragged into the Western World War Three scenario that seems to be forming.

In terms of change, Biden has proposed a $3.5 Trillion infrastructure package. According to Senate Majority Leader Charles Schumer, *"Every major program that President Biden has asked us for is funded in a robust way."* Because of the way Congress and the MSM function, the true nature of all the programs might not be known for years.

However, it has been noted that inflation is increasing. In accordance with Reaganomics, a package that increases the National Debt from $28 to $32 Trillion sounds scary but can be meaningless if all the money is spent during the current Biden Administration.

Reaganomics would anticipate a period of double-digit inflation would start with the next administration. That would monetize the debt and, effectively, make it meaningless.

If the interest on the debt is at the July 2021 30-year Treasury bill market rate of 2%, as interest goes up, the market value of the treasury bill will fall. This is then augmented by the inflation-driven decline in the purchasing value of the dollar. When taken together, the Treasury can buy back the debt for pennies on the dollar.

In short, the National Debt is part of a monetary Ponzi scheme that will defraud any who purchase Federal securities.

As with his border policies, Biden is being a good Reagan Republican.

CHAPTER Six - Define Yourself to Yourself

While others are always defining us, we define ourselves through the way we control the definition imposed by others. We also do so by defining how we work with ourselves – how we impose control over our actions and work habits.

At birth, we emerge from the womb programmed to seek the approval of our parents – specifically our mother who is the source of nourishment and nurturing. Society is structured to reinforce that bond throughout our lifetime; it is only after the first five to seven years of life that we begin to bond with our father – or the male role model in our life and society.

When I was a kid, I had a rule: "*Always play by the other guys rules. When they lose they have no right to complain.*" If the rule was followed, they usually lose, and can never win.

It's a quid pro quo variation on the Golden Rule – "*do unto others as they do unto you*" – they are competing against themselves; so we can laugh if they "lose at their own game."

The Golden Rule is not some silly Bible thing, it is a very real part of daily life and experience that can be found in the fundamental doctrines of every culture.

Between 1955 and 1959, there was a TV sitcom base on the adventures of Master Sergeant Ernest G. Bilko – an expert at manipulating the military bureaucracy, who also conducted gambling operations. Formally, it was entitled The Phil Silvers Show, but we kids knew it as "Sargent Bilko."

In one episode, Bilko quotes a segment of the bible to the Military Chaplin – who is surprised Bilko would know the Bible, much less be able to correctly cite chapter and verse. Bilko then looks the Chaplin in the eye and applies a military dictum – you need to "*know your enemy.*"

Bilko was both expressing a "Golden Rule" variation and saying you always consider the other guys' rules as part of your operating strategy.

To understand how someone is to treat you, you must know the rules they play by. And to defeat an opponent, learn the rules they play by. In sports, you might want to have a copy of their playbook.

Bilko was a professional soldier; the audience were those who, only a decade earlier, fought in World War Two; two years earlier, they or their sons had fought and died in Korea.

Until then, war was accompanied by a common assertion – *"God is on our side."* When we watched Bilko, God was not part of the game. We came to understand, Bilko knew exactly who he was, what his occupation was, what he was doing, and why.

Within the context of the times, Bilko defined himself to himself and did so within the context of the way others chose to define him – never losing sight of who he was and what his job was. There was no doubt Sargent Bilko was a leader that his men trusted. We knew why they trusted him and why they were happily followed him.

If you are a leader, you know exactly who you are, you understand your rules and the rules you are expected to play by – knowing these things, you can become a James T Kirk who must 'beat' a Kobayashi Maru scenario.

The combat simulation was designed to be unbeatable – it's a rigged game. The only way to survive the Kobayashi Maru scenario is to re-rig the rigged game. As Kirk said, "I changed the conditions of the test!" And that is exactly what we all must do in a life-or-death situation – it's your opponent's rules which must be broken.

Back in the 1970s. I noticed as people reach their third quarter-century, religion takes on importance. When you are in your 70s, death is a real and inescapable possibility. With death, you will learn if the mythical afterlife exists. Until death, it is a thing with which to control dim-witted types – they must find religion or go to hell.

Religious writings and mythology take on meaning. But that is because they contain wisdom – and the religion involved need not be the Western ones. Eastern religions offer a great deal of wisdom without the need to threaten. They do not need the fear of eternal punishment. Rather they teach calm and the love of life in all its forms.

In a world where life expectancy is 75-85, people reach a point where they instinctively recognize the way the universe works. There is a wisdom that comes at the point of transition – and it demands we consider that reality that governs how the universe works.

It is a different form of leadership.

The elderly are leading themselves. They are viewing the universe and all of existence as the herd they will be running with – it's not a stampede; you can't lead the herd, you are part of it. And the goal is to run longer than the rest of the herd, but you must also accept that you might not achieve that goal.

Emperor Constantine violated everything Christian, but on his deathbed be confessed his sins and converted. The basic idea, which still survives as a tenant of Catholicism, is that – if you confess before you die, you can be absolved of past sins, and if you commit no sins after the concession, you go to heaven.

Thus, those who intentionally commit genocide, or who intentionally violate all the scriptural prohibitions shall be fully absolved and are welcomed in heaven. Thus, we see the wisdom of Constantine, who waited until the last possible moment before he converted and confessed. It is Constantine's legalistic joke – kill all those you wish ... then convert and confess ... you will join the faithful in Heaven and avoid Hell.

At the end of life, we consider such legalistic games. The joke is that these are the same games we play with taxes and the planning of our estates to avoid inheritance taxes. The only difference is that we do it on the gamble that there is a Heaven or Hell.

Constantine illustrates a talent of timeless leadership. It is the idiot who dismisses things. The true leader considers all the possibilities and then hedges their bets.

Consider the idea expressed by the French philosopher Blaise Pascal (1623–1662) – specifically what has come to be known as "Pascal's Wager." The shorthand version is that you can believe or not believe in GOD (screw the religions). If there is no God, disbelief costs you nothing; if there is a God, disbelief costs you everything. So the safest bet is to believe in God.

Supporting the belief is simple semantics – God is a term assigned to the beginning, to the point where nothing becomes something – the state before the "Big Bang". Thus, in scientific terms, God exists – it's the religions that appear to be bullshit.

In terms of "Pascal's Wager," we attribute some intellect or purpose to the state of being called God. Does the Universe obey consistent laws? Is there a possibility that science might eventually discover what Albert Einstein called a "Unified Field Theory" – a formula that unified all events in the universe?

Should a rational leader dismiss the possibility of a single mathematical expression describing physical interactions that occur in a non-sentient universe?

Is there a God?

How did a beginning emerge from absolute nothing?

Is there a mathematical logic governing the universe?

Do the laws of nature apply to humanity in the same way they have been shown to apply in science?

Pascal determined it was safer to bet on the science.

Comically, that decision predated the science, but it was based on the simple logic of a wise man being the one betting on the no-lose position.

Define who you are. Are you wise enough to go with the no lose proposition? Can you translate that theoretical wisdom into your daily life?

Are you in control, or are you being controlled?

If you want to know who controls you, look at who you are not allowed to criticize. But realize that the most intelligent people are willing to criticize their own actions – and then learn from knowledgeable criticism.

And therein lies another point of leadership – leaders are those who have learned to appreciate knowledgeable criticism. That means they accept the negative, then challenge the critic to provide the positive alternative – that challenge proves that the critic is based on knowledge and not simply contrarian with a hope of being correct.

When they look around, the intelligent person marvels at the efficiency of life. A scientist expresses it as Conservation of Energy and will tell you there is no waste because everything is recycled.

When faced with religious doctrines involving a Heaven and Hell, scientists and intelligent individuals will dismiss the idea as inconsistent with the observed evidence.

Since it is inefficient, a wise person dismisses the idea of eternal torment in the context of a demon overlord punishing souls – it is a total waste of both forms of energy.

On the other hand, a leader might choose to acknowledge the concept but change the context. They would define souls as pure energy and therefore something to be used to keep some aspect of existence functioning. But what?

Hell is defined as a fiery place – a place of eternal fire or heat. Shall we look into the sky at noon on a beautiful day and exclaim *"quod erat demonstrandum!"* And then assert that Hell is not below, it is above. The souls of the damned fee the nuclear reaction that contributes to life.

Immediately the leader brings together two concepts – the observed science, and a religious threat that controls moral behavior, to allow for the existence of both. The fun part: Can the naysayer refute the assertion by providing another source for the energy at the heart of every Star?

Thus, a "scientific" premise allows for eternal damnation or punishment in a way that does not require mythical demons.

If the universe reuses everything; if it uses organic waste to create compost that is the fertilizer for new growth; If we breathe in oxygen and exhale carbon dioxide, then plants breath the carbon dioxide and exhale oxygen, is there not a synergy to life so that each form benefits the other? And if so, it is the job of the leader to identify that synergy and use it to dispel myths – or find the good in things perceived to be bad.

If we can, as nature demonstrates, establish a combined interaction between two or more forces that have an effect that is greater than the sum of their individual characteristics, then we have the basis for bipartisan action and a winning agenda.

When we replace the Luddite mentality with Progressive thought and creativity, we can create a positive outcome. That is the job of a true leader. Illogical superstition is the basis of all Luddite action; therefore traditional "organized religion" can be challenged and eventually abandoned – as happened with a worship of the ancient pagan deities.

How do you define yourself?

Are you aligned with pagan superstition or would you say you subscribe to rational thought that is consistent with the demonstrable evidence of the universe?

Easily a third of all humanity subscribes to some form of pagan superstition. They follow without thinking. And when faced with a "religious' doctrine that promotes thought or logic, they traditionally attack its adherents – hence we see Western anti-Semitism and a fear of many Eastern religions where the focus is on physical wellbeing. You might want to think about the laws the State of Alabama had against the practice of yoga or meditation.

From 1993 until May 2021, Yoga was part of the culture war and under Alabama Law, "*Chanting, mantras, mudras, use of mandalas, induction of hypnotic states, guided imagery, and namaste greetings shall be expressly prohibited."*

Maybe it didn't matter that *"Studies have shown that yoga helps children cope with daily stressors."* Maybe, as we have already discussed with the link between intelligence and stress in pre-school children, the ban was explicitly intended to help dumb down Alabama students – by increasing their stress levels.

Of course, some might say it was a Constitutional issue of Church-State separation derived from the fact that *"Yoga is a practice of Hindu religion."* Accordingly, the state still bans the traditional *"Namaste"* {"I bow to you"} salutation.

In the above quote, we see the mention of *"induction of hypnotic states"* and *"guided imagery"* – both are techniques for the lowering of stress and improvement of attention spans or cognitive thought.

As a societal norm, former slave states are known to be opposed to education and the development of intelligence. The year 1740 saw passage of the first laws against slave education implemented in South Carolina. Anti-education laws recognize that education breeds knowledge of an alternative to their state, so slaves would seek freedom and an elevation of their status.

This prohibition was contained in Articles 44-49 of the 1740 Slave Code of South Carolina. And because escaped slaves were a problem, it also authorized that *"for every scalp of a grown Negro slave with the two ears, taken on the south side of St. John's river, the sum of fifty pounds."*

In many ways, restrictions on income – a below poverty minimum wage – and a tax system that sees the wealthy pay a lower percentage their income than the poor or middle class, are the means by which the slaves are controlled.

To restrict education one need only ensure it comes with an excessive cost or lifelong debt. The excessive cost can be in the form of local property taxes, and the lifelong debt is student loans for necessary higher education. Since basic education benefits the nation as a whole, its costs should be part of the national budget. And, if higher education produces a greater taxable income, it too should be covered by the Federal budget.

President Biden proposed covering two years of higher education. Those supporting modern slavery will go on record in opposition to the proposal – or find a way to bury it.

Obviously, there are different types of leaders. Those who oppose free education will also oppose other things that are a benefit to both the nation and the average person. These are leaders who want control by reducing the majority of people to powerless subjects and are most apparent when seen in a failed "Socialist" context. Those who want to advance society appear to be "socialists" but we see their people prosper and advance.

In a society where the people prosper, we observe there are higher taxes, but lower out-of-pocket after-tax costs. There is a strange result – all of the desired necessities are provided and the after-tax disposable income is higher among those who appear to be more heavily taxed.

In the words of the Johnny Cash song, "*Sixteen Tons*," the modern goal of the would-be slave masters is to place the average American in a situation where they "*get Another day older and deeper in debt/Saint Peter don't you call me 'cause I can't go/I owe my soul to the company store.*"

What the true social leader wants is to lift people up and remove the basic fear of financial instability or dependence.

Again, this involves the lowering of stress and "*induction of hypnotic states*" and "*guided imagery*" in a form that serves to expand mental ability. But, as a society, we often consider such tools to be humorous.

Take the example of two TV characters "Sheldon Cooper" – who comes in two forms, the adult on "The Big Bang Theory" and the child presented in the prequel series "Young Sheldon" – and then the police detective comedy character, "Monk."

In both, we are presented with high IQ individuals who demonstrate oddities of focus or behavior. In the case of Monk, the focus is on an obsessive-compulsive disorder also see in the character of Sheldon.

It has been claimed the basis for Sheldon's character is a variation on Asperger syndrome – which normally manifests with social interaction and nonverbal communication issues, as well as narrowly repetitive patterns of behavior and interests. If that were the case, then it would also apply to Monk.

In fact, what is being displayed by the fictional characters is an exaggerated variation on typical high IQ behavior, where the lack of social interaction skills is directly related to the fact that such interacts are generally non-productive. This reality is also manifested in normal business environments as complaints about routine "staff meetings."

Curiously, we might being seeing examples of this high IQ behavior in President Biden's avoidance of normally routine press conferences or occasional short-tempered response to a reporter's infantile gotcha-type question.

TV audiences find it comical whenever high intelligence individuals invoking an instinctive form of self-mesmerism, or *"guided imagery."*

The TV characters are engaged in a form of self-hypnosis designed to enhance their thinking. In the case of Monk, it is accompanied by the positioning of his hands when viewing and recreating events at a crime scene. The placement of his hands in his visual field serves to focus attention in much the same way the use of the camera focuses your attention on aspects of the scene – revealing only that visual information called for in the script.

In daily life, self-mesmerism is a means of calming the body and focusing the mind. Since it is achieved by establishing a routine, most of us subconsciously know we routinely try to get people to engage in self-mesmerism – we simply phrase it with the suggestion they should establish a daily routine for any of the behaviors they wish to encourage. Maybe it's spending time sitting with a cup of coffee, or setting aside a fixed time for their daily exercise regime.

The goal is to enhance focus and productivity.

Background sounds in the form of looped musical tracks, or certain types of music, also enhance productivity. But, as we noted with fetal development, disruptive, loud, and fast-paced music create a disruptive mental rhythm.

Over time, and through repletion, self-mesmerism will create the mental equivalent of muscle memory – the response becomes instinctive. The wrong stimulus can induce a negative pattern that can counteract the benefits of a high IQ and can completely destroy those of average intelligence. Conversely, a proper stimulus can raise a person of average intelligence to a superior productive level.

Monk's hand positioning, Sheldon sitting in the same location on the couch, having a cup of coffee or tea at a specific place on your desk, all serve to create the repetitive pattern that enhances the thought process through the elimination of all the usual secondary distractions.

In the latter stages of the Covid pandemic, an increase in telephone solicitations served to introduce disruption; this then caused an increase in annoyance levels; low-grade stress levels increased to the detriment of the immune system or the ability to "work from home."

Whenever low-grade stress increases, so do stress relief through acts of violence. {Rip-apart an important document, Break something, smash your fist into a wall, or attack another person.}

Because stress is a natural part of the environment, some leaders gear their activities to include routinely random stress elements.

As was noted in the Trump card series, President Trump

liked to litigate – he welcomed the stress of a court action.

While it might seem ridiculous to most people, there are people who thrive on different forms of stress. In some, this makes them natural combat soldiers – having experienced combat, and their inner stress reaction manifested itself, peace drives them crazy. Others, as mentioned by Young Sheldon, are happiest when they are taking exams or undergoing some form of high-stress testing, or problem-solving experience.

Some are leaders whose technique is to create chaos or social disruption. They create an enemy – an "other" – who serves as a common point to rally the masses.

History reveals this with the anti-Semitism within the Roman Catholic Church. And its transference to the Protestant doctrines that, eventually, culminated with the KKK and Nazis.

In 1290, Britain's King Edward I issued an Edict of Expulsion that, while not officially repealed, remained in effect until 1656.

To some degree, Shakespeare undermined the edict – in 1604 he produced the Merchant of Venice, whose premise was built around established Jewish Mercantile tradition and Italian anti-Semitism expressed in laws targeting Jewish Doctors.

Jewish Doctors were more competent than their Roman counterparts, so Italy had enacted laws that made it a crime for a Jew to spill the blood of a Christian. Shakespeare used this as a focal element in the Merchant of Venice – it was the law that Shylock would violate by demanding his pound of flesh.

The period broadly classified as the Spanish Inquisition created a situation in which Jesus would need to renounce the basic faith he followed to worship himself through the power of Rome. Hatred for Jews and Muslims ruled the period and enhanced the power of the Church.

However, the effect was to create support for Columbus, establish colonies in the Americas, and undermine those forces supporting the Spanish economy – Jews moved to Portugal and made it a mercantile power. Then they entered Holland and by the time of the Pilgrims, Britain recognized the benefits of a merchant culture. It also helped that King James assumed the throne and, in 1603, unified the Scottish and English crowns.

The British remained anti-Semitic well into the start of World War Two. But, because Hitler had sought to expel all the Jews from Germany, we forget the British reality, the rise of Zionism that it spawned, and American anti-Semitism. Since no nation would take the Jews in, Hitler initiated the Holocaust.

Traditionally, adherents to the Hebrew culture served as the ideal "Other" – because of the mercantile tradition that dated to the time of King David, though their numbers were always small, Jews were universal and an economic elite.

With the emergence of Covid-19 and the vaccine, the Star of David – in the yellow star design utilized by Hitler – became an anti-vaccine badge sold by a Nashville, Tennessee hat shop. The Star contained the declaration "Not Vaccinated" and had been reported being worn at anti-vaxxer demonstrations in the UK and Germany.

Why would the anti-vaxxer movement – those knowingly dismissing medical science and exposing themselves to deadly disease – be associated with those who went through, or died in, the Holocaust?

Was the symbol intended to associate Jews with deaths resulting from a lack of immunity? What was their leadership thinking?

When an incompetent leader needs a universal enemy, the perfect enemy is either rich or represents a different belief system (religion or culture). In some cases, false leaders seek to establish parallels between a historically oppressed group and their movement – it negates the need to present and argue the merits of their agenda. In other instances, they will boldly lie about the merits having been presented – we saw this in the first Trump Impeachment, where Representative Adam Schiff routinely declared "*overwhelming evidence*" of Trump crimes, but at the Senate Trial, he could produce nothing.

To create chaos or social disruption it is necessary to find ways to divide the people. False leaders will intentionally create disorder as part of their process. Often, as in the Case of Schiff, Pelosi, and Schumer, they will lie about the underlying facts – declare the beauty of the *Emperor's New Clothes* and accuse those who cannot see it of being stupid and unworthy.

There is a leadership class that emerges to offset those who thrive in chaos. These individuals are recognized by their ability to take personal attacks in stride. As I mentioned in the first of the Trump Card series books, Donald Trump is such a leader, and he seems to have taught the style to his children.

As I warned, those who want to disrupt Trump could not be successful by mindlessly attacking him. Trump thrives on attacks. As a result of their chaos-driven approach, we had two impeachments without evidence or a factual basis. Even with Trump out of office, we see mindless attacks based on his taxes.

Problem! Trump has been routinely audited by the IRS and generally goes out of his way to remain within the wording of the law. Trump Tower is the product of Trump turning to the State to demand the City obey the law – as written.

Since Trump is accustomed to running with and taking control of the stampeding herd, the way to overpower him is to stop the stampede. When dealing with a leader like Trump, as I warned, the first thing you do is accept whatever is rational.

Trump wanted the Border Wall. But Trump's Wall was just an improved version of Obama's "Secure Fence." So attacks on the Wall were an attack on Obama – which, comically, is exactly what Biden's policies achieve.

Biden's policies are those of Ronald Reagan.

To put it mildly, Biden is teaching us how you present yourself as one thing while behaving like the exact opposite.

As a result, we have returned to the illegal influx that was the result of Reagan's open border policies; we are hearing calls for amnesty and legal pathways to citizenship for those who violated our immigration laws. And, in terms of the nation's finances, Biden's first budget carried record deficits that would transcend every election over the ensuing twelve-year period.

Thus far, Biden's leadership style is proving to mask the reality of his objectives. At the same time, if the cost-benefit economics are rational, the appearance of a deficit and national debt problem might prove illusionary.

Biden seems to have defined himself to himself in a way that works. We know Trump has a long history of adhering to his self-definition. In Congress, in both the House and Senate, we have people like Pelosi, Schumer, and AOL who are defined by their ability to say NO and support chaos.

In contrast, at the end of May 2021, Senate Leader Chuck Schumer had no problem standing before reporters to declare his difficulty getting things done – because all the Republican members of Congress were "*under the thumb*" of Trump.

Imagine the level of leadership involved or underlying the "matter of fact" Schumer statement.

The image being promoted by Schumer is that of a twice impeached single-term President, whose business activities were currently under investigation by the New York Attorney General, exerting more power than any of the Congressional leadership or other former President.

Is Schumer an idiot? Or is he describing a Machiavellian tactic being used by Trump?

Schumer's myopic partisan approach to those identifying with Trump's base demonstrates a lack of basic leadership skills and when he realized it, he downplayed the tactic.

On 29 May 2021, Schumer's move to form a 6 January investigative committee fell apart. Schumer's objective was to continue the attacks on Trump and avoid meaningful legislative programs. The process serves to distract the media and public from any partisan harm Schumer intends to promote.

Schumer's agenda-style was supported by his approach taken to the bipartisan legislative amendments put forward by Maine's Republican Senator Susan Collins. Collins suggested several minor procedural changes that would improve the basis for and functionality of the Commission.

Upon announcing the vote, Schumer made it a point not to mention Collin's, and it was only after the vote failed that he chose to mention that he supported Collins' amendment. Since the point was moot, his statement was a political nod to his base – allowing him to later claim he supported Collins' suggestions.

Schumer's actions ensured the Senate effort to create an independent investigative committee would fail. As a result, the matter bounces over to the House where Pelosi is free to create a partisan select committee to investigate or manipulate the facts to generate whatever biased outcome is necessary to shape the 2022 election.

Those who cannot lead through honest efforts and goals will do so by selecting an enemy and then persistently lie about reality. Unfortunately, their efforts seldom result in something positive for their constituents.

This means there are times when we are the recipient of the work of others. All too often the recipient is the one blamed for the actions of a predecessor or third party.

In many ways it is an emotional *"Butterfly Effect"* – we know the storm, but have no knowledge of the butterfly having flapped its wings. Or, we do know about the butterfly but fail to see or acknowledge the causal connection.

When we have instances where the responsibility and all relevant blame should reside with the one currently in power, one common strategy is to blame a predecessor. When dealing with the crisis along the Southern Border, members of Biden's administration attempted to blame Trump. But, as we saw with the impeachment assertions, they could not provide any factual basis or support for their claims – they simply presented the gullible with an opportunity to accept the wondrous beauty of *The Emperor's New Clothes.*

When Donald Trump became President, his past persona was redefined by those he defeated and whose control over the masses he threatened. By the time we heard the 2020 results, we had forgotten that Hillary Clinton said she was cheated and the election was a fraud. We also forgot that AOC and others were calling for the elimination of the Electoral College. Trump forces took up that call, and the 2016 claim of election fraud, to say Trump was the President.

The arguments being put forth by Clinton's people were not being echoed by Trump's forces. Trump forces were simply playing by Clinton rules and by doing so they were able to add power to a possibility that Trump would repeat what Glover Cleveland had previously achieved – being elected to separated terms, and thus having two distinct administrations.

Because Glover Cleveland had established the possibility, there was a realistic possibility that Trump could duplicate the event. That possibility is supported by the record incumbent vote received by Trump, and the fact that he went from no electoral experience to President in one try – whereas Senator Biden took three tries and a stint as Vice President under a man whose border policies he immediately contradict upon taking charge of the Oval Office. As a result, we have the Border Crisis and what appears to be a return to Reagan Era policies.

Throughout his career, Biden has been defining himself – in many instances as a bigoted opportunist promoting those things which are in the worst interests of the nation. That said, he is still demonstrating a common form of leadership. Leaders often represent narrow special interests over what is best for those who they are leading.

While the idea of a suicidal lemming is a myth, people do tend to behave in a suicidal manner and will follow orders that lead to their own death. In times of war, the idea of "self-sacrifice" has been know to save lives. But we need only look to terrorist suicide bombers to see instances, where the only thing achieved, is mass murder that motivates others to turn against the underlying movement.

Many politicians function under the premise that only the short-term outcome matters. They recognize and accept the premise the average person functions on short-term memory. Unless the information is repeated, it is not internalized, as a result, we find a basis for advertising and propaganda or some forms of political presentation.

The Nazi, Joseph Goebbels, defined it as the"Big Lie": "*If you tell a lie big enough and keep repeating it, people will eventually come to believe it. The lie can be maintained only for such time as the State can shield the people from the political, economic and/or military consequences of the lie. It thus becomes vitally important for the State to use all of its powers to repress dissent, for the truth is the mortal enemy of the lie, and thus by extension, the truth is the greatest enemy of the State.*"

Because the concept is familiar to many, we see it being subliminally invoked by referring to Trump in the context of his "Big Lie." Only the "lie" is found in the words of those asserting that the possibility of election fraud promoted by Clinton was impossible in 2020. They avoid the fact that Trump had only rebranded Hillary Clinton's post-election position – then they impose a subliminal trigger phrase, the Nazi "Big Lie."

They also avoid the fact they called for the elimination of the Electoral College – because it functioned as intended in both Trump's and Biden's Electoral College victory.

In that context, are you a player or the one being played?

Recognizing the value of repetition, P.T. Barnum is cited as saying: "*I don't care what the newspapers say about me as long as they spell my name right.*"

Trump thrives on the Barnum approach – it defines his

career and the basis for his real estate empire, which is based on the prominent placement of his name on his properties and, whenever it was possible, in the entertainment media.

Barnum died on 7 April 1891 and Goebbels was born on 29 October 1897, which places the expression with Barnum, and propaganda realization with Goebbels. But the Old Testament makes it a point to repeat important laws or guidelines three times, so the reality is ancient.

Barnum recognized the public will remember the name but, not the context. Therefore it does not matter what is said about the individual, so long as the name is clearly stated.

When demeaning an opponent it is important to be vague about what they have "done." The goal is to attach a vague negative to the name recognition – assert *"overwhelming evidence"* in the absence of evidence.

To defeat Trump, you play the Karate master and use his own weight against him. You do that by moving in the direction he is going and then exerting lateral pressure. But, Trump is a propaganda Karate master and has ways to "sidestep."

Since the stampeding herd by standing still in front of it – that's how you get crushed – more time devoted to Trump by MSM, the less is available for his opponents. Trump shaped the debate – he identified it as a "Witch Hunt," an act of mindless superstition devoid of factual basis, devoid of *"Overwhelming Evidence"* of anything. After two impeachments, there has yet to be a statutory citation to support either a High Crime or High Misdemeanor.

Of course, that did not, and can not, prevent the ignorant from marveling at and describing the wondrous beauty of *The Emperor's Clothes.*

How do you define yourself? Just how beautiful are the clothes worn by those who would be your leaders? What about your clothes – were you, like the Emperor, told you had some on?

CHAPTER Seven - DEADLY LEADERSHIP

Biden assigns Harris the border crisis and exposes her complete lack of leadership abilities. On 2 June 2021, The Examiner produced a story headline, "Kamala Harris is in over her head and embarrassing herself," and there is little doubt that she is in well over her managerial head.

However, saddling her with the task she cannot address was a wise move for Biden, who created the crisis by turning on his previous boss, Barack Obama, and opposing the Secure Fence that Trump to make truly secure and so re-identified the Fence as a Wall.

Of course, President Biden is motivated by deeply rooted self-interest motivations that have resulted in his desire to serve the interests of Pelosi Democrats; curiously, this means being a Reagan Republican in his economic practices and all border-related policies.

During the 1980 campaign, Ronald Reagan stated that "Rather than talking about putting up a fence, why don't we work out some recognition of our mutual problems? Make it possible for them to come here legally with a work permit, and then, while they're working and earning here, they'd pay taxes here. And when they want to go back, they can go back. They can cross. Open the borders both ways."

With those words, Reagan emphasized the alternative to a fence was allowing Mexicans or South Americans to legally obtain work permits. His audience was Houston, Texas, as it existed on 23 April 1980 and, with Reagan's victory, the next 20-years saw a steady increase in illegal crossings.

The illegal mass migration influx ended with the security increases that followed the 11 September 2001 terrorist attack and the Fence became a funded policy when Senator Barack Obama successfully promote the 2006 Secure Fence Act – a law and appropriation of funds that Representative Nancy Pelosi voted against.

Then, as President – with Biden as his Vice President – Obama began to build his Fence. But the Fence was just that, a rather weak, easily passed, physical barrier combined that was with a series of car barriers. During construction, and to ensure it worked psychologically, a series of policies accompanied the fence; they were designed to persuade illegals that there was no reward associated with the risks they were taking.

As a builder, Donald Trump understood the difference between a Fence and a Wall. More importantly, he understood that done properly, a Fence was a Wall – a Wall did not need to be made of mortar and stone, it did not need to be a "Hadrian's Wall" or "The Great Wall of China." Even more important, Trump knew that the Chinese wall had actually failed to achieve its designed purpose, so he continued the Obama policies.

When Biden was elevated to POTUS, one of his first acts was to cancel Obama's Fence and open Trump's Wall to give us the Reagan open border policy that Pelosi supported. Open the southern border before Climate Change began to drive more people north. Reversed Obama-Trump border security policies, created a Border Crisis to complicate matters at a time when the nation was already disrupted by the Wuhan Coronavirus.

Biden shattered a migratory dam and the resulting flood quickly reached and by April 2021 exceeded pre-9/11 levels. As stated throughout the Trump Card book series, Climate Change goes beyond the simple matter of CO_2 or any other climate gas levels associated with Industrialized nations using antiquated carbon-based combustible technologies.

The issue of Global Warming is related to population – 2,000-years-ago, an author of the Book Revelation projected that our century would see a third of life die.

With the Change in Climate, and an enormous human population disrupting a natural recycling process – the balance of Nature – we are now in the process of recording species that are going extinct.

We are also approaching the point where the post-World War Two surge in population, the Baby-Boom Generation, has combined with Baby-Bust to culminate in reproductive neglect or parenthood postponement that defines the Millennials. The commutative effect is, by the year 2050, when the last Boomer would be 85-years-old, the human population will be about a third of its peak numbers (which have still to be determined).

Consider the three factors: a global Baby-Boom, that is combined with excessive heat in the region 15-degrees latitude north and south of the equator, and a mass migration of people who traditionally live within that equatorial expanse.

Civilization emerged in the Northern latitudes between 15 and 30 degrees; our modern civilization emerged above 40 degrees north. As humanity moved north, diseases were given the southern regions to evolve in. The autoimmune disease, HIV, emerged at 11 degrees north – in Nigeria.

Coronavirus is a culling virus, Plagues are diseases that are deadly in their own right and occur in areas where humans have yet to develop a natural immunity – smallpox falls into the category of a disease that is prevented by another disease, cowpox. In a world that has evolved to maintain balance, most diseases have a natural vaccine or natural remedy.

Cowpox is a disease that protects against a more harmful disease; in the African or African-American community, sickle cell anemia is a genetic problem – but only because its carriers were removed from the malaria regions where it evolved as the body's natural defense to the more deadly problem.

The Covid-19 type virus culls the herd of those who are already at death's door. Climate Change will be introducing the type of tropical virus which kills on its own.

As the CDC weekly numbers revealed – when matched when compared deaths from all causes in previous years, all the pandemic has done was expedite those deaths that would have occurred likely have within six months and been enumerated in the comorbidity categories.

The pandemic issue is more of a cultural transition and social mobility issue – it is helping to achieve social evolution before the Climate Change plagues emerge.

In the age of Covid-19 and the various pandemic events that will accompany both animal and human climate migration, it is worth looking at the period of the Roman pandemic of 165 to 180 AD. Known as the Antonine Plague, or Plague of Galen – as named for the physician who described it – has been cited as the first pandemic in recorded history.

Exactly what disease was involved is undetermined, but the leading contenders are either smallpox or measles. There was a later related Plague of Cyprian, 251 to 270, which might also have been one or both of the diseases which were finally eradicated by the discovery and perfection of vaccines in 1749 – around the time America's Founding Fathers were being born and the world was entering a new phase in its social evolution.

Rome created an expansive culture that gave rise to the Frankish Empire. When Rome imploded, the seeds planted by the critical leadership cultures came together to yield the hybrid culture that emerged with the Christian variation on the ancient pagan religious beliefs and traditions that became a foundation of the Frankish assumption of Western leadership embodied in the emergence of Charles Martel "The Hammer," (688–741).

The Hammer's grandson was Charlemagne, "Charles the Great," whose descendants emerged as the catalyst for modern history, various aspects of Western Culture, and leadership.

As the map on the rear cover shows, until 1444 Europe was a hodgepodge of independent feudal monarchies existing under a Holy Roman Empire – call it the original version of the European Commonwealth, but with far more members. As the map shows, about five regions approximate modern times.

With the fall of the Roman Empire, Italy was reduced to

a Papal State; the Scandinavians, the Vikings, had evolved into the Normans and controlled Britain; in 1492, Spain destroyed itself by combining global expansion with the expulsion of Jews who had helped define its evolution since the time of King David.

The year 1492 saw disease go global – European diseases infect Native Americans, Caribbean diseases infect Europeans, and Asian diseases came into play as travel times were reduced from years to months, weeks, or days. This introduced the era of the Black Plague; our modern era of air travel and Climate Change driven population shifts, that will likely bring another plague or pandemic before 2038.

Now add the concept of a "Leadership" that is dedicated to minimizing stress and ensuring the "General Welfare" – the "Health and Welfare" of the nation. This leadership must lower "societal stress levels" and requires a homogeneous population.

Within that context, we find two types of leaders – those who are forgotten and those who are remembered.

Historically, there are many noteworthy transition points – few of them are associated with real people: Aryan India and the Indus Valley Civilization produced Indo-European culture; the Hyksos, or "Shepard Kings" of Egypt produced the Moses, the Exodus, and then Biblical Hebrew culture. We remember the Twelve Caesars of Rome; Temüjin's Mongol Empire served to alter China and separated East from West 200-years before Columbus.

Prior to 1492, the Chinese already had trade ships that were larger than anything available to Europeans. The largest Chinese junk was comparable to a football field and could easily carry all three of Columbus' vessels. But China restricted its travels to its area of the world – where it defined trade terms.

A shorter trade route between Europe and Asia held the promise of shifting the mercantile trade balance of power – and it did. It created the British Empire. But it also made possible the survival of infected merchants and their crews who had previously died in transit while experiencing what we could call a social distancing quarantine before they could infect others.

As we know, the Black Death was related to fleas on rats transported as unwanted passengers on merchant ships. There had been a bubonic plague affecting Afro-Eurasia between 1346 and 1353 – which was a period of change for sailing vessels. It was a period when single mast ships were transformed into the twin masted Carrack or "merchant ship" and a change in sail design similar to that used in China.

As ships travel faster and shortened the social distancing or isolation period experienced by sailors – when travel times are shorter than an incubation period, the disease spreads more rapidly. This was the driving force behind the spread of Covid-19 via Europe.

Unnecessary production of goods in another nation can be the driving force behind the next plague. Our leaders will need to repatriate production and control the borders before that plague becomes self-evident.

Were an enemy to create a disease, any weakness or lack of border control could decimate the nation. Every nation will need a modern form of Ellis Island medical check. To whatever extent it is possible, a nation needs to be energy self-sufficient. It also needs to be technologically self-sufficient.

We need to avoid a new variation on smallpox infected blankets that were given to Native Americans. Genocidal germ warfare worked and will work again.

The events in Europe that gave rise to the Pilgrims also saved them from the Great Bubonic Plague outbreak in Europe. It was also known as the Black Death and Black Plague; in 1625, it became the Great Plague of London. This was 18 years after the Pilgrims – a religious group known as the English Separatist Church –abandoned England and relocated to Amsterdam and the town of Leiden in the Netherlands {Holland}. The Pilgrims then came to Massachusetts in 1620, so escaped the effects of the Black Death that killed over 10% of Amsterdam's population between 1623 and 1625.

Individuals run out of fear of an occurring horrific event – Leaders tend to recognize the early signs of an emerging problem and guide their people to safety. Leadership displays intelligence. Knowing that, is it any surprise that, in 1636, they founded Harvard?

The Virginia colonies were first established in 1607 and were mercantile oriented. In the Biblical tribes, the merchants support the scholars; accordingly, in 1619 "Henricus Colledge" was chartered; in 1693, The College of William and Mary was established in Williamsburg, Virginia.

The British colonists focus on education and within 12-years established places of higher education. New England's population continued to add universities and prospered. The Southern Colonies were agriculturalists whose leaders kept the education to themselves. That difference continues to define the regional differences.

While the Spanish arrived in 1492, they took 57 years to establish schools in Mexico City, Mexico, and Lima, Peru. The Spanish were invading conquerors looting the population of its gold while converting them to Catholicism.

What we are looking at is a foundation for the differences between various patterns of leadership and the long-term effect on the resulting indigenous culture. Latin countries focused on religion and narrowminded profiteering; Southern states were founded on illiterate agriculture; New England focused on education and mercantile traditions. Plagues or pandemics like to travel with merchants but kill the less educated.

The history of Rome can help us stand outside ourselves.

We know Rome was, like the Spanish, a brutal and highly exploitative empire. Part of the Roman process involved the use of "slaves" – in modern terms, low-wage migrant workers

– in the context of an imperialist power that stationed its military forces in territories outside its borders or lawful jurisdiction. It was also a governmental entity that had its origin in migration, in asylum, and traded on the incorporation of the foreign – be it foreign ideas or workers. What we view as modern American Progressive Liberalism is little different from the Marxist ideas that caused the cultural revolts in the late 1840s; then brought the 48ers to the United States where their ideas joined with those of Harriet Elisabeth Beecher Stowe – reflected in Uncle Tom's Cabin (1852) – and ideas of Abraham Lincoln. Both of whom were in their mid thirty's when Marx and Engels were writing the principles that demonstrators were dying for in the streets.

As the pandemic or plague pattern shows, be it Rome in 165, Europe in 1350 and 1620, or the current world situation, the pattern of technological change, plague/pandemic, and the call for social change that come together.

It's been said the United States is a modern incarnation of Rome during the period of the Twelve Caesars. And in that mode, decisions will be made that shape both the Empire and the future. But, as true leaders know, when there are major troubles that need immediate attention, major decisions must be made. At the same time, if cultural elements strive to trouble the mind of the leadership, those major decisions should not be made. To do so means those decisions will be tainted by short-term emotional factors.

Curiously, President Biden seems to void the problem by avoiding the media – or passing the issue off on Vice President, Kamala Harris. In analyzing the tactic, we have possibilities of high competence or gross incompetence. Either through some display of wisdom or incompetence, after being placed in charge of dealing with the Border Crisis, Harris avoided the usual Press Conferences where politicians state their positions and goals, or some proposed initial steps to evaluate the situation.

However, the Democratic administration faced a bigger

problem of their own creation. With Trump, they trained or rewarded the media to be a far more aggressive attack dog than was normal. With Biden – whose campaign approach was to hide in his basement – we see the realization that dog doesn't care who it attacks. The media has devolved into a wolf that eats its prey. As Biden understood, it needs to be avoided. If it cannot be avoided, then you tread carefully and, as we have seen Biden do, if it looks like it's about to growl, you wack it with a "Bad Dog" comment.

The result is a headline like the one that appeared on 8 May 2021: "Snarky Biden Snaps At Reporter Who Asked About Mask Use." The day before, Biden had been asked about mixed messages on mask-wearing – do those who are vaccinated need to wear one and specifically why he continues "to wear a mask so often when [he's] vaccinated and [he's] around other people who are vaccinated."

His response was simple: "Because I'm worried about you." And, while he said it in a serious tone, Biden took a beat and then added: "No, that's a joke. It's a joke."

He then restated the question and went on to explain: "Why am I wearing the mask? Because, when we're inside, it's still good policy to wear the mask. That's why. When I'm outside – and the problem is: Lots of times, I walk away from this podium, you notice, I forget to put my mask back on because I'm used to not wearing it outside. "

Members of the Jewish community would recognize his explanation as consistent with Orthodox practices designed to avoid the accidental violation of the Laws; philosophers would see it as the underlying premise for "Pascal's Wager" – always take the position with the lowest adverse consequence, the one that will, ideally, cost you nothing and give you everything.

But the real display of leadership was the "that's a joke" – which declared to the reporters that he doesn't give a damned about them or their health. He's viewing them exactly the same way Trump did – MSM has become the problem complicating the real problems.

Symbolically, MSM functions as a political Covid-19 and Randolph Hearst was its first recognized outbreak – since the Hearst created military conflict, MSM exercised its disruptive powers at every opportunity. As we said before, their motto is, "If it bleeds it leads;" when there is no blood, they create it.

As Texas Republican Representative Rep. August Pfluger stated in March 2021, President Trump "knew what the source of the problem was. He was working with those [Northern Triangle] governments, making sure that the [migrant] surge didn't happen."

Situated in the Western hemisphere, Northern Triangle nations are roughly 15 degrees north of the equator and ideally located for the incubation of diseases emerging from equatorial latitudes.

Thus pandemics apply to the type of leadership needed by any nation intent on making it a 21st-century leader.

Whatever side of whatever political divide you identify with, you cannot just lock up the other side or put gags in their mouths — there's far too many of them. Add to their numbers the fact that the internet and other emerging communication technology have provided the basis for instantaneous seamless coordination of activities, and the common enemy is one that refuses to take a side.

Advancement requires leaders who strive for bipartisan objectives. Those who oppose are worthy of being followed only if they can clearly show the factual error in the proposed goal or policy. Try asking the "Cancel Culture" advocates why it is wrong to remember the past and honor those who stood for what they believed in – even if future events clearly established they were on the wrong side of history.

They cannot do it and therefore are not worthy. Worse, they violate the time tested idea that those who forget history are doomed to repeat it. No qualified scientist would erase all records of the failed experiments. What they do is learn from them, they ask why it failed, and why a different variation on the experiment succeeded. And why they have a success, the first thing they want to do is have someone else duplicate their experiment – to ensure it was valid. History is our teacher.

You should want to know what people you don't agree with are saying, and you want to know what people you don't respect are saying. You cannot understand the argument lies if you are not aware of the logic or strategy your opponent has committed to.

As we know, MSM is committed to "fake news" – the act of misrepresenting events to place them in a negative light – as opposed to being truly objective and presenting the logic behind the news. If a crime is committed, and the perpetrator is from a minority race, the race will be prominently displayed in the headline or paragraph lede.

MSM enjoyed the pandemic ride – after the election, it was a great filler. As expected, MSM has failed to report any analysis of the numbers as filed by the CDC weekly data. If they did, they would see the pandemic has killed those who were already due to die from those routinely recorded medical issues.

Granted, the total number of deaths from all causes has increased relative to previous years, but that only reflects aging baby boomers – those born between 1946 and 1965 turned 75-years-old in 2021. At the beginning of 2021, the average life expectancy for American women was 81 years and for men 77 years. On average, pre-War Silent Generation individuals should already be dead and half the Boomers will have died before the 2024 Presidential election.

Therefore the death numbers for 2020 are augmented by remaining Silent Generation members and will continue to be augmented. Consider the number of famous people who are in line to be part of that count: Joe Biden (78), Nancy Pelosi (81), Clinton Eastwood (91); and the "Golden Girl" Betty White (99).

We can search MSM obituary reports and realize how many have died natural deaths during the pandemic – and by doing so added to the total deaths. Third world death tolls reflect the generally poor state of health in those "off the road" nations. And, it follows that their numbers will increase even as the Industrialized nations declare victory over Covid.

The dominant factor in the spread of disease is regional contact –merchant trade routes and speed of travel. The China virus came to the United States because China supplies the USA with both its hi-tech – its computers, cellphones – and medical supplies. Executives and company representatives routinely fly between the two nations and therefore can spread disease in its incubation period.

The pattern of spread directly reflected trade relations in the early stages of the Wuhan outbreak – early foreign outbreak regions were those in new active negotiations with China. This was followed by the spread to nations with established trade.

As time went on, secondary markets became exposed – these markets dealt with the exposed or infected nations. Then, in 2021, the infections increased in regions like India, where the virus began to spread from the industrialized Northern regions into the Southern areas (much like the virus spread from New York to Florida and then across the nation).

Leaders need to address the spread of disease in terms of commercial trade routes and supply lines. While the virus first entered in California and Washington State, because commerce centers around New York – Wall Street, International airports connected to Europe, and a broad range of commercial sector headquarters – that was where things became the most serious.

As was recognized early – as mentioned in the first of the 2020 Trump Card series books – the New York leadership had gone out of its way to prove its incompetence. But, because the Governor's brother is a major commentator for CNN, MSM shielded New York from responsibility.

The first case of Covid brought in from Europe should have resulted in a quarantine policy. Instead, we saw Covid-19 cases deposited in elderly care facilities where it spread to those who would prove to be its primary victims – those who were already past the average life expectancy or fighting to stay alive.

From the old age facilities, it spread to the families who visited and the staff caring for the residents. Because the staff tends to be "minority," Coronavirus quickly infected minority communities and from there was spread to all the areas where their skills provide the shadow support for the city – craftsman, janitors, building staff, and other "essential workers."

As the virus vanishes, as the vast majority of the nation's population joins the "herd immunity" pool, we expect the death rate would continue to climb. As the numbers reveal, Covid-19 has nothing to do with it – it's just a change in the causal record for those who would have died within six months anyway.

Since the Boomers' peak birthrate fell in the period from 1957 to 1961, it follows that death rates for men will peak in 2038 and for women, it will be 2042. More importantly, the deaths deemed natural or from all causes should climb at a rate that is roughly parallel to the Baby Boomer birthrate history

Are we going to see leaders who recognize that reality?

If they do, they will be promoting programs that allow for the growing number of elderly and take into account that any improvements in medical care and availability will serve to delay deaths and enhance a general need for reliable retirement income.

America needs a Universal Basic Income – a permanent economic stimulus targeting and applying to those over 65 – which can serve to augment their Social security income. If it were implemented by economically competitive leadership, the program would be, in terms of citizens, truly "Universal" and it would be equal to an amount that is 125% of poverty.

The effect would be to neutralize or eliminate the need

for welfare, while also imposing an economic preparation for the next pandemic.

If this means some people will not work, that only means those who do can be paid more. Thanks to Covid, we are seeing many employers raise base wages beyond the highest minimum wages in the nation – in many locations the starting wage can exceed twice the state minimum wage.

The nation needs leaders who refuse to display or hold a slave-owner mentality. Slave owners covered food, clothing, medical, and residential costs. They denied their people any disposable income or means of becoming independent. It was the logic of "the company store" – the idea that the wages are so low that the worker is trapped by debt and says "I owe my soul to the company store."

We entered the pandemic with welfare subsidizing places like Walmart. But by February 2021, Walmart announced it was going to raise the wages for 425,000 of its employees above $15 an hour – though it would retain the $11 an hour starting wage. They did not eliminate the basis for the governmental welfare subsidizing wages, but, thanks to activist pressure, they did that the first step.

With competent leadership in the House and Senate, the nation would is a permanent base level economic stimulus that provides a solid economic foundation, and eliminates the need for the Federal and State expenses associated with welfare, eliminate the need for a personal deduction on Income Tax forms, while also protecting the economy from the economic disruption of another pandemic resulting from immigration caused by Climate Change driven migrations.

As an added bonus, the UBI cash benefit enhances sales and profits, increasing both the Gross Domestic Product (GDP) and both corporate and personal tax revenues.

Done by competent leadership, economically, the UBI is a no-lose action being tried in some states.

CHAPTER Eight - BURY THE LEDE

Leadership.

What is it?

What writer's style or technique can be used to bury the lede on leadership?

It's actually quite easy.

Just require the reader to pay attention and think. As a rule, people do not like thinking. They prefer to be told and then to obey.

Thinking requires that you define their terms and then define the objective or the goal to be sought and reached. Any rational goal that is sought will be reached.

Do you need to lead the nation, or is it sufficient to lead a State, or maybe just a County or City?

Maybe you want to lead a company or a division within a company? These are career goals and are joined by "career achievement" markers. In the *"Big Bang Theory"* TV series, it was Sheldon & Amy Cooper winning a *Nobel Prize in Physics*.

A fictional character leadership achievement concluded the series. But the idea is real. The idea that you can be as good or better than anyone else only takes on real meaning if it is punctuated by an established achievement recognition.

In tHe real world, in 2019, Nobel academy member Ulf Danielsson opened the awards presentation with: *"The whole universe was in the hot, dense state, then nearly 14 billion years ago expansion started."*

Those familiar with the TV show will recognize these words as the opening line of the show's theme song, which the secretary-general of the Royal Swedish Academy of Sciences, Goran Hansson, acknowledged was a nod toward the "fantastic achievement" achieved by a show which brought the *"world of science to laptops and living rooms around the world."*

Leadership achieves multiple things. It can produce a long-running TV series, a prequel spinoff, and bring a positive element of the real world into the lives of the average person.

Throughout his career, Donald John Trump was clear in his goal to have his name remembered – which means ensuring that your name is known. As a real estate developer, he placed his name on every structure or property. And when he achieved recognition, the entertainment media would capitalize on that name recognition by inserting his name into their scripts.

Trump was mentioned in the TV series *"Sex in the City"* as being symbolic of wealth – the man the wealthy turn to when they need money. Trump made a cameo appearance in season two and a voice-over commend from the series character Carrie Bradshaw says, '*Samantha a cosmopolitan and Donald Trump, you just don't get more New York than that.*'

In the popular TV series "Charmed" [S6; E21 2004] they had a demon make an off-the-cuff remark about Trump having a TV show – it was the first season of *"The Apprentice."*

When Trump became President, there was the infamous editing out of his cameo role in the 1992 film *Home Alone 2*. But the reality is that Trump had promoted his persona to the point that he had cameos in dozens of films and TV shows – in addition to those shows that simply referenced him.

Leadership can take the form of being a PT Barnum. As the history of the print media shows, from the earliest reporting days, one thematic stance has always been taken by those who seek recognition: *"Boost me or knock me; it doesn't mean a thing. Just make sure you spell my name right."*

As I mentioned early in the Trump Card series, and as all have seen after he became President, Trump is very comfortable with attacks – they get his name in the media and spread his fame. He lives on the adage of our joint youth, *"If you want your book to sell, get it banned in Boston."*

When alcohol was made illegal, drinking increased; when

abortions became legal, the number of out-of-wedlock babies increased, and, in terms of the percentage of fertile women, the number of abortions fell – Bible Thumpers lost one of a favorite means of attacking young women.

Attacking something is often the best way to promote it – attacking creates a false image of holding *the moral high ground* and hiding your daily immorality. Leaders understand that. Fools will keep attacking when they should be "accepting."

The true leader attacks only that which is demonstrably detrimental to their goal, and harmful to society.

As seen with the Inquisitions and witch hunts, religious groups attack harmless tradition and that which is beneficial to society. Among Islamic groups, rather than build Palestine we see poverty used as an excuse to attack Israel – using money that could place Palestinians among the richest people.

Some leaders lead so they can destroy their followers. We see the nonsense promoted by BLM; the facts are that when it comes to killing 81% of white deaths are at black hands, and 97% of Black murders are also at Black hands. Police killing Blacks, only 1%; whites are three times as likely to be killed by police. In terms of Fact-Checking, it was documented by USA TODAY on 29 September 2020.

Again, we can look to leaders like Martin Luther King Jr, who denounced the practice of black protestors destroying their communities – now repeated by BLM demonstrators.

Poor Leadership is a function of leading a mob opposing some social or economic interest. All leadership manifests as positive or negative, saintly or demonic. Demonic elements are preparing society for World War Three – due around 2033.

The key to leadership is exposed or embodied in youth like Greta Thunberg who, when only 15-years old, became a global leader on Climate Change and its control.

Now 18, Greta is firmly at the forefront of the Climate movement and demonstrating that "*The sins [or wisdom] of the fathers are visited upon the children"* into the third or fourth generation.

While Greta is the product of individuals who pursued the operatic arts and acting, her line includes her Nobel Prize-winning second cousin, Svante August Arrhenius, whose focus was the climate issues Greta is now pointing out are upon us.

In scripture, the third and fourth generation is 57-years from the adult source whose mode of thinking and traditions were taught parent-to-child, then to the grandchild, and finally, possibly to the great-grandchildren.

This was seen in the Biblical story of Exodus – Moses causes the tribes to wander the desert for 40-years. During that time, pragmatic experience teaches new traditions to the young, while the period ensures the original Exodus generation would die off – we are told their natural death was the 40-year goal.

The Baby-Boomer generation will be with us until 2050 and we are being governed by their Silent Generation parents. That's what happens when life spans double.

When I was 35 and researching data for a book, I was surprised to learn that, globally, I had already outlived half of those who were born in my birth year. In the nearly fifty years since then, global life expectancy has doubled. Because we are also having children later in life, the *"sins of the fathers"* can be expected to span more than 114 years – rather than about 57.

Leadership decisions made in 2021 will shape the world until some time after 2200. The emerging leaders of today are the ones who are pouring the foundation those future leaders will build upon. Greta Thunberg is among those attempting to ensure the foundation is properly situated and poured. Social Media believes Trump's Atlantic City corporate bankruptcy is more important.

Given Greta's climate stance, disruption of the electrical grid in places like Texas, the flood causing rain's in Europe, and the record heat waves that will only get worse over the next two decades, would seem more important. Biden promoted vague, costly, improvements to our infrastructure; Trump suggested the "Border Wall" – which Biden opposes – be used as a solar energy platform capable of providing for most of the nation's energy needs. Texas could pay for a solar installation, and by maximizing production, sell its surplus energy to the national grid system. What do Twitter posts focus on?

The closest Texas is coming to fulfilling the ideal is a 16 June announcement that it is dedicating $250 million toward completing the Border Wall along the 1254 mile expanse shared with Mexico.

Biden's Border Crisis in full swing, and the focus must be on Obama's Secure Fence and the goal of true security it would provide. In the meantime, on 17 July 2021, the media reported the first two cases of Monkeypox arrived in Texas from Nigeria.

For now, a CDC spokesman claimed, "*Monkeypox is a rare but potentially serious viral illness that typically begins with flu-like illness and swelling of the lymph nodes and progresses to a widespread rash on the face and body.*"

But it also marks the first "*rare*" tropical disease to reach America – it caries a one-percent fatality rate, and requires no co-morbidity, and is not a Covid-19-type culling virus.

Texas leads the nation in renewable energy projects. The Texas geography is ideal for solar and because of its oil fields, it has a reputation as an energy producer. When Covid-19 first moved west from China, it impacted energy-producing Iran – has Monkeypox chosen a similar route through Texas?

California and New York promote open borders because their leaders seek non-voting cheap {slave} labor who serve to gerrymander their representative counts and milk the rest of the nation for Federal welfare funds.

When the Constitution was being written there was a debate over "Free or Slave" and how a non-voting slave could be counted for representation of those who can?

The answer was, they would be fractional people – free women couldn't vote, but were full people. Their racial group was not an issue, females and children could not vote, and slaves were non-citizen property. Property cannot vote, but non-citizen humans needed to be counted.

The British leadership introduced the 1806 Foreign Slave Trade Act which prohibited British slave trader operations in foreign territories. The following year, in nan attack 9on the Triangle Trade, the purchase of African slaves was forbidden. The industry was then given time to adapt and, 26-years later, on 28 August 1833, the Slavery Abolition Law eliminated all slave trade.

The date, 7 April 1837, is related to the Hans Christian Andersen tale, "The Emperor's New Clothes," which tells us that people will see what they are told to see, or what they wish to see. Today we witness it as *"The Big Lie"* that holds there was Russian collusion in the defeat of Hillary Clinton, but no false ballots, miscounting, or errors, in the 2020 election.

It is an eternal truth: *"It's easier to fool people than to convince them they have been fooled."*

Variations of that quote seem to be a popular variation on the 1647 Baltasar Gracián observation: *"Every blockhead is thoroughly persuaded that he is in the right, and every one who is all too firmly persuaded is a blockhead, and the more erroneous is his judgment the greater is the tenacity with which he holds it."*

In 1906, Samuel Clemens – Mark Twain – incorporated the idea in the observation: *"How easy it is to make people believe a lie, and how hard it is to undo that work again!"*

As periodically shown by governmental administrations or those who would-be leaders. The common element appears to be that they forget, or willfully ignore, where the culture has been and where it is heading – they often focus on the cracked edges of the road, while ignoring the pothole in front of them –

or even the reason for the road's existence.

Evolution, change, is the hard center of the road. Those who talk of intelligent design are the same ones who deny the existence of that design. They assert a perfect creator – that the architect of existence is infallible – yet they rejoice in a process that is focused on what they call errors. Their "perfect deity" is too stupid to have designed a perfectly imperfect universe– a universe that is just out of balance enough to keep it in motion.

Then there are the "science" supporters. They too are in denial about the overall nature of evolution. They deny that which can be, and often is, called "socialism." But socialism is the idea that we should balance both ends of the economic and social scale. If we fail to do that, the "Perfect Design" will cast us away – as it has every creature that has, ultimately, gone extinct.

The only real difference is that humanity has the tools of its own extinction and appears to be happy to use them. If that is not true, explain nuclear weapons and other weapons of mass destruction. Or, maybe, explain the belief and determination that the Coronavirus originated in a Wuhan lab.

It makes sense that there are biological laboratories that are exploring the nature of viral life; are exploring how it can be controlled; might even be considering weaponization. Those who hate themselves and their culture are the first to deny that the latter is a possibility. They also deny that the source of the virus could have been laboratory carelessness.

If we roll back the clock to the era of Martin Luther King Jr., we see warnings of the stupidity demonstrated by burning their community or destroying Black-owned businesses in those communities – while also shouting that Blacks are being denied the right to prosper. Those who cheer the demonstrations are seen as being pro-Black supporters of Black Lives Matter.

This is not unique to America. It is a universal pattern of behavior. Muslims wave the Koran – which demands that a good Muslim never harm an innocent. Then they tie bombs to children and send them into marketplaces where those bombs are triggered – killing innocent Muslim women and children.

Koran-waving Muslims violate the prohibition against suicide and take pride in committing that violation through the act of murdering the faithful on pilgrimage to Mecca.

The 9-11 suicide was nineteen Saudis wanting to murder as many innocents as possible. Its effect was to grant George W. Bush an opportunity to begin a "war" designed to overthrow a competitor of his Saudi oil partners, murdering millions of innocents over the next nineteen-years. A secondary effect was the long-term damage to the American economy.

"How easy it is to make people believe a lie, and how hard it is to undo that work again!"

There is the idea: *"Thou shalt not kill."* And we see it is those who wave the Bible the most who are always the strongest advocates of WMD development and deployment.

We are taught our beliefs and select our leaders based on the effectiveness of those initial teachings. Those who would be leaders must first determine who they wish to lead; then they must devote their souls to that constituency's belief system.

On 13 June 2021, Joe Biden defined the goal and reality that is connected to this aspect of leadership – when dealing with the opposition or those whose belief indoctrination is different – *"There's no guarantee you can change a person's behavior. Autocrats have enormous power and they don't have to answer to a public. The fact is that it very well may be that if I respond in kind, which I will, that it doesn't dissuade him – he wants to keep going."*

Hum, note the *"respond in kind"* – that is the traditional *"Do unto others AS they do unto you."* Interestingly, it works. When pushed, there are three choices: accept being pushed, you push back, or you resist long enough so that you can then step aside and let the idiot fall past you ... maybe even on their face.

Biden has told us the first option is not acceptable. The question then is, which of the other two will be the game? Are we going to see a pushing match – something like a pair of equally matched Sumo wrestlers?

Or does Biden push just enough to get his opponent to fully commit to pushing back – then we'll see Biden step aside and the opponent rush past only keep going and ultimately fall, so Biden wins?

Biden needs to hold the Democrats in line, face in the proper direction, and then when the Republicans rush past they are doing so in the wrong direction – defeating themselves. If we look at the leadership demonstrated by Pelosi and Schumer, we see the Democrats have followed a path that's headed in the wrong direction – so what is Biden going to do?

For his first 120-days in office, we saw that the focus was fixed firmly on Trump. Democrats and the media were clearly showing they were still afraid of the guy who had left the ring.

Or. If they were not afraid of Trump, maybe they wanted him back – he was the adversary they knew how to attack; the one that would stimulate a record voter turnout based solely on the goal of his defeat.

An intelligent approach, mentioned early in the Trump Card book series, would be to support that which is deemed worthy of support. Something is worthy of support whenever it resonates with the desired target demographic or offers solid merit over the long term.

Those who have seen old interviews are aware that when Trump responded to early suggestions he run for President, he was more relatable to the Democrats than Republicans.

Of course, that changed during the Obama era, when the Republicans leaders decided to play the Birther game while also suggesting that Senator Ted Cruz, a "Natural Born" Canadian", was Constitutionally eligible to hold the office, while they were simultaneously arguing that Hawaiian born Obama was not.

As some are aware, this display of cognitive dissonance was addressed in my 2013 book, *"President Ted Cruz: The 2016 Election and America's Future."*

It was that point in history when Donald Trump realized he had an opportunity to take charge of the Republican base.

This realization gave rise to the infamous 2016 assertion: *"My people are so smart – and you know what else they say about my people? The polls? I have the most loyal people – did you ever see that? I could stand in the middle of Fifth Avenue and shoot somebody, and I wouldn't lose any voters, OK?"*

Trump's people have proved loyal – hence the sustained fear among the current idiotic and self-destructive Democratic leadership. As for being smart, the Republican base was tired of the cognitive dissonance that treated them like idiots and, as Trump realized, there was a similar response emerging within the Democratic ranks.

However, as shown with his third attempt to introduce a Constitutional Amendment to outlaw flag burning – in June 2021 – Montana's 58-year-old GOP Senator Steve Daines might be too young, or too stupid to know the matter had been settled around the time when he was a toddler.

Of course, in our context, it might also be that he believes the Republican Baby-Boomer base was not aware of the Hippy Vietnam War protests involving flag burning, and he's counting on those younger than himself to be aware of the reality that the law could not stop the symbolic protests.

It wasn't that they couldn't yell it should be illegal or that "Free Speech" allowed it – thereby creating the necessity for a Coonstitutional Amendment. NO! The reality was rationality – how do you, respectfully, discard an old and tattered flag?

The only proper way to dispose of a flag is by burning it.

Daines' Constitutional Amendment would require that a tattered flag be tossed in the trash. Then, where ever the trash is disposed of, if they burn their trash, would need to sort through the garbage to remove any flags; clearly, a failure to do so would violate the Constitution.

But the dump could just bury the flags along with any cat or dog shit. Daines' action shows he is devoted to creating the best way to desecrate the flag. In effect, Daines is ensuring the desecration of the flag, and any voting for the constitutional amendment joined in that desecration. It's a neat way to show they secretly hate America.

If the issue is people using the burning of the flag as a symbolic swipe at the nation is what is to be addressed, a leader would offer a resolution or law stating the flag MUST be burnt as a sign of respect for any flag that is to be disposed of. Then they would also insert that anyone who burns the flag has done honor to the flag and is showing their deep respect and love for the nation.

The Hippy-era Flag Burning photo-op is suddenly turned into a symbolic demonstration of love for the nation and its ongoing policies. And the media can be made to be obligated to report it as such – or be on record creating "fake news."

Leaders ignore the "*oh but*" possibilities by turning any action that can have two valid, but conflicting, interpretations into one that is positive for their cause. And, ideally, they do so with the support of a tradition that affirms their interpretation.

The best form of Leadership is a constant in the process. For most people, being attacked is a deterrent. For a stallion, being attacked is how the herd gets to see you as their leader.

But remember and keep in mind a basic reality. The one who is regularly attacked is the one at the forefront of the war.

To be truly successful, be number two to number one, but not in the line of succession. Number one will be knocked off and his successor step in – to then be attacked. Number two is the servant who stands just behind the throne and has no interest in occupying it.

In the corporate world, you want to be the indispensable person who heads up a critical department. In many firms, the most powerful person is the boss's secretary or head secretary – as it was after World War Two, today it may be the head of IT.

As the fear he stirred among the Silent generation has taught us, Donald Trump is a special case. He is interested in history and not short-term profit. Where Pelosi was attacked for having a $24,000 refrigerator, people are attacking Trump when he [allegorically] loses his. Trump's bankruptcy filings are mentioned, but not the fact that he walked away with tens of millions in cash flow while all around him simply went broke.

The "Lede" is, unless your goal is to be remembered in the history books, be number two – and lead. Or, choose the alternative – step aside, do something you enjoy and/or can be proud of, and enjoy life. Lead only when necessity forces you to step in, take charge, long enough to get things back on track.

That might mean standing up at a school board or town hall meeting. It might mean temporarily taking the lead as the chairmen of a committee or, maybe, the whole group. Do what can be done and then return to your true interest.

Nobody demands you make history. Sometimes, as with George Floyd, the undeserving get center stage and occupy the historic spotlight – then they become a footnote and forgotten.

When we bury the lede we lower the focus on the historic reality that patterns repeat. As my readers know, I am prone to repeat a basic observation: *"Everything is the same, they just change the name and order of magnitude."*

We can conclude this chapter by asking if I successfully buried the lede.

CHAPTER Nine - Cycles Repeat

Cycles are cycles because they repeat. They might, like waves hitting the shoreline, vary in magnitude, but they always have a defined rhythm or pattern.

Leaders are aware of the rhythm and their presentation is tuned to it; when they establish a melody, it resonates with their target demographic. The more pleasant or relatable the music, the larger the audience demographic response – you get a song that's a hit. If you're really good, you create a classic.

As with music, some leaders design presentations that are calming or restful – MSM would call them dull and boring. But boring works. As we know, MSM thrives on excitement or blood in the streets.

Boring does not sell advertising or increase viewership.

Sudden shock and aw will grab attention, but it does not hold it. Only the slow and persistent threat of a shocking event will hold the MSM audience. Impose enough stress and comic entertainment will rise – comedy without a message will draw any captured by and seeking escape from media-induced stress.

Politics follows the same pattern.

Donald Trump promoted "America First" – standing tall and strong against the economic and radical forces gathering to threaten society.

The threat? Pick one or all and add a few more: Climate Change, Chinese economic expansion embodied in a "New Silk Road" initiative, terrorists who kill for the sake of killing – as demonstrated by the great and unnecessary harm they do to their own – and the issue of border security that was recognized by Senator Obama in 2006; then acted upon when he became President in 2008.

Obama represented the culmination of a transition into a new era. When the Constitution was written, the opposition forces were well enough entrenched to force its inclusion into the National Charter. The Racism we identify was not systemic to all of the people. In the years before and after, leaders of the nation had loving relationships with members of other races – Elizabeth Warren could assert Native American roots because intermarriage was common in the early colonial era.

It was so common, Mitochondrial DNA Sequencing in several British port communities has revealed significant Native American ancestry – colonial-era sailors or merchants brought Native American females home to Britain.

Given the number of Spanish Jews who arrived with the first wave ships lead by Columbus, and the fact they ran north when the "Church" started to arrive, the Indian Tribes in the Southwestern United States might well show DNA identified as Sephardic Hebrew.

And while relationships might not have involved lawful marriage, they were common enough to ensure there are very few Black Americans whose DNA is not partially European. As for Native Americans – they don't dare base tribal membership on DNA, because a large percentage of theirs is also European.

After his wife died, Thomas Jefferson entered into his infamous relationship with her enslaved half-sister. There were members of Congress who maintained similar relationships – one even relocated west so he could legally marry his love.

But, because cycles repeat, this is no surprise to any who have read the story of the Exodus. When the Israelites entered their promised land, the first thing they were told to do was to slaughter the men and any women who had "known" them. The remaining virgins were to be taken as wives.

By keeping the virgins, was Israel founded on rape? The story tells us the people violate the order and allowed some of the natives to live and either become part of the tribes or a future threat to the nation.

MSM both reports and ignores the numbers of illegals who cross the Southern Border. And why not? MSM reports on the numbers so it can claim credibility; it ignores the reality by avoiding discussion of the ramifications. Those who talk of those ramifications are generally classified among racist or the right-wing.

From the viewpoint of MSM leadership, the fact that the migrants have no employment, do not speak the language and lack basic educational skills needed to obtain employment that is not welfare subsidized serves their "Bleed-Lead" mentality.

The Biden Administration opened by initiating a border crisis. The media avoided emphasizing the degree of trouble it promises to create over the next two decades.

Nearly sixty-five thousand individuals are stopped every month – we have no idea how many get through and enter the country. We can point to many causes for their migration, but the one inescapable driving force, that will be with us into the next century, is Climate Change.

If we look at maps showing both heatwaves and water shortages, we see the Southwest – where these migrants could be expected to settle – is suffering the greatest impact. This is not going to change for the better. As Humphrey Bogart once observed: *"Things are never so bad they can't be made worse."*

The migrants represent an invading army numbered in the millions. They are the Israelites – but without a leader or cultural code of conduct. They are the Spanish Conquistadors bringing an alien culture to the region; they might even bring as yet to be identified tropical diseases.

Given the cultural and economic goal conflicts seen in the Biden Congress, is the nation ready for the impact of those who have yet to recover from the damage done by the Spanish four-hundred-years-ago?

Look at the streets of San Francisco, the area comprising Nancy Pelosi's Congressional District.

What you'll see extreme poverty, vast numbers of homeless are living on the streets – with or without tents – it is a district marked by extreme poverty and hardship which Pelosi and her ilk have done nothing to address.

Pelosi, along with her political demographic, wants to add to those numbers. Their form of leadership cares nothing about the average person and even less about those in dire need of assistance.

What they do care about is "body counts" – living people who can be counted in a census and those increase the number of Representatives allotted. Ideally, that body count relies on non-citizen, non-voter, underage, individuals who would have no meaningful voice to raise against those who profit through ignoring their needs.

Consider this: Pelosi supports open borders, and that has resulted in unaccompanied children flooding in – assuming they are given the right to stay, they need to be educated.

San Francisco's Unified School District (SFUSD) is the seventh-largest school district in California and educates over 57,000 students every year.

Based on preliminary Customs and Border Protection data for March 2021, 18,500 unaccompanied children crossed the border. That equates to tripling the size of San Francisco's every three months – if the kids were sent to Pelosi's district, do you think San Francisco would welcome the additional cost on top of the $300 million currently allocated?

The Rhythm of Leadership can be based on the level of dim-witted in the base demographic. With the naked Emperor standing before them, how many will describe his exquisite new clothes?

We can get a rough estimate by counting those in San Francisco who have voted for Nancy Pelosi, those in New York City who backed Chuck Schumer, and those who voted against Donald Trump's "America First" – voting against Trump, rather than for Biden.

Elections are a traditional form of leadership choice.

History books proclaim the United States to be a new form of government, a newly evolved selection process, that was markedly different from the past. But both representative and democratic forms of government go back to the pre-Roman Age of Greece. And when we consider Moses or King David, there are hints of the electoral choice process in the Old Testament.

There is also a reality that, while some leaders emerged through their fighting skills, most leadership is based on either the ability to take charge in a time of crisis or through winning personalities and personal popularity in more relaxed times.

For some, Leadership appears difficult. But all a leader does is define a goal or destination and then pick the direction that should get his followers there. Everyday life is far harder.

OK. Maybe you haven't thought about it.

Consider that every destination has the option of return. Some goals or destinations are for resettlement, others are transitory – deployed soldiers will eventually come home. But, while they are deployed, they advance towards the goal and if something goes wrong, they have an option to retreat.

In daily life, every day is spent striving to go from today to tomorrow – and if things go wrong, there is no retreat.

There are no do-overs, but corrections can be made.

When you make a mistake learn from it, and keep moving forward. When you learning from a mistake, you can avoid repeating it. But, remember, part of the learning process is determining what went wrong. But, it is not an error but missed opportunity to achieve a goal.

When you evaluate the error, first determine if the goal was valid. If the goal is invalid, the failure could be academic. But, if the goal was valid, its validity did not end with the failure of one approach.

We are moving from today into tomorrow. It doesn't matter if you sit on your butt or actively determine to advance. There are only two possibilities, you will either evolve or die.

Evolution means changing traditions and perspectives.

The cycles will repeat – but with variations.

Traditions must be placed in perspective. We saw this in the story of Noah when it points out that *"the men of renown"* were believed to be the grandchildren of God who were born to mortal women via the sons of the creator father.

The tradition did not end in the period associated with the flood fable. The idea of direct worship of "the father" did take root. But, as we know from Christianity, there were whole cultures that could not abandon traditional beliefs; as a result, they replaced the deity sons with the father and then repeated the ancient tradition which the story of Noah was intended to end.

When we seek the beginning of the attempt to end those claiming a divine right to lead, we find it a mythical Flood that is dated to a period thirty-five hundred years ago. But, the flood failed to be reality and the Divine Right of Kings persisted – all that happened was that they started to shift the power to the Church or Organized Religion.

As a result, we see that those who wanted social justice were placed in a position where they attacked the Church – the attacks are then attacked as a denial of God, which is the name given to the beginning of all things.

God is the modern name for what the ancient Egyptians called it "The self-begotten beginning" – which is, when you push them for the way we get something from absolute nothing, is what scientists or physicists will call that initial event. When it comes down to it, every evolutionary theory of creation begins AFTER there is something to evolve from.

Karl Marx is said to have been "Godless." Yet if we look to the *"Communist Manifesto"* we are told, *"Law, morality, religion, are to [the proletarian or member of the working class] so many bourgeois prejudices, behind which lurk in ambush just as many bourgeois interests."*

Three elements critical to society have been subverted to control the average person: "*Law, morality, religion.*" When the Constitution was written, taxes were to be paid by, were the responsibility of, the landed gentry. But when the Income Tax came into existence {1913}, Tax Laws were skewed to allow the rich to escape payment.

Morality? Do you recall the last time you witnessed any morality in government? Not the false and hypocritical claims of morality – the Right to Life which will mandate a woman die rather than have the abortion that will save her life, or will force a child to be born so it can have a name on the tombstone that will mark its grave within two years of its birth.

Do you see Moralists demanding that every pregnancy be accompanied by full and free medical care?

Are the moralists demanding proper care for children?

On that point, what do we know of their history? There is the historic assertion of opposition to birth control but, for 280 years – from Pope Clement VIII, in 1599 until 1878 when Pope Leo brought an end to the practice, Popes approved of the ultimate birth control, the castration of prepubescent males.

They did it, created *castratos* because they valued choir singers more than they did children or the Commandment to "*go forth and multiply.*" The very act of castration had the effect of murdering many of the young boys "*thou shalt not kill*" – except when creating a choir singer.

In 1900, you could beat a child to near death.

In the 1977 Supreme Court case of Ingraham v. Wright, the use of corporal punishment in schools was deemed NOT to be a violation of the Cruel and Unusual Punishments Clause of the Eighth Amendment. While states across the Northern segment of the nation, and along the west coast, have banned it, school corporal punishment practices are still legal in southern states.

Child labor laws removed the ability of employers to use

corporal punishment, but what about parents?

There is a serious question as to the rights of parents to do what a school teacher can lawfully do. But the real issue is moral leadership. What is the morality of corporal punishment and why is there such a variance in leadership – could it be that society or humanity deem it moral and proper to harm others?

While there is no necessity for a direct connection, it is worth noting that views on child cruelty and slavery have run in a parallel direction. Of course, in the American South, the child could also, literally, have been a slave owned by their parent.

All life reproduces to ensure the survival of their species. Sentient beings reproduce to ensure genetic continuity and eventual genetic dominance of their species. As part of that search for dominance, we see reproduction resulting from lust.

However, slaves were once related to reproduction – the Harem, concubine, and mistress, in an environment where the women had a status in which one was placed above the others – slavery was economical.

Cultures would identify by class or caste and identify individuals based on their degree of freedom in service to the *"bourgeois."* A few pages from now we will see that Karl Marx identified the caste system by his focus on the lowest level of the working class, which he labeled the *"proletariat."*

The term *"proletariat"* has its origins in ancient Rome, where it was a reference to wage earners with no value beyond their ability to work and their children were generally listed as property – their only capital assets.

Marx took the term *"bourgeois"* from the French where it originated as *burgeis,* the term for a walled city in which all trade and commerce were based – the cities were owned by the nobility and originated as an extension of castle fortifications.

The *"proletariat"* are slaves for hire, therefore, must also provide for their own survival. In economic terms, they tend to be far cheaper than slaves who are property. This cost reality was not lost on the British and those in the Northern States whose livelihood was derived from commerce rather than daily agriculture.

In 1822 – four years after Karl Heinrich Marx was born – British parliamentarian Richard Martin pushed through a law banning certain aspects of animal cruelty. As mentioned, that was the same era when the British started to outlaw slavery. If you recall the *"Give me the child,"* you realize that this was also the era in which the adult mentality of Marx, Friedrich Engels, Bruno Bauer, and Max Stirner {born Johann Kaspar Schmidt} was born and defining philosophies that are still studied. There was another man born in the era of change we identify with the Germans – Abraham Lincoln.

Another individual associated with that "counterculture" group was Friedrich Wilhelm Nietzsche – among his statements is: *"That which does not kill us makes us stronger."* As for those who would lead: *"Whoever fights monsters should see to it that in the process he does not become a monster."* When it comes to methodology or the imposition of beliefs upon others: *"You have your way. I have my way. As for the right way, the correct way, and the only way, it does not exist."*

Born in 1844, Nietzsche witnessed a failed social reform movement that gave rise to the 48ers. That failed attempt at European social reform brought the movement to America and influenced both the thinking and legal practice of Abe Lincoln.

Change crosses generational boundaries – *"Sins of the fathers"* – as seen between 1828 and 1898 when several states passed anti-cruelty laws that protected animals and also freed slaves. Animal rights gave rise to children's rights.

The first legal case involving child abuse was Mary Ellen Wilson, in 1874. This was the same year when The New York Society for the Prevention of Cruelty to Children was founded – it was they who sponsored the Wilson Case – which was won with the argument that children were animals and therefore covered by the Animal Abuse Laws. That is, their argument was based on the connection created in Darwinism.

Isn't it comical to think that those who argue creationism are arguing against an evolutionary connection between child animals and humans – effectively they are, arguing to exempt children from the protections afforded animals?

With the proper presentation, Laws can be subverted to mean whatever you wish – since they are just another form of animal, and animal cruelty law protects children. But what if Animals and humans are created separately, without any real connection other than some designer deity, then the two are no more related than a human is to a plant or meteorite. The basis for the Wilson Case goes out the window and the dominoes are free to fall as they will.

The *"bourgeois interests"* are tied to profits – where is the profit? Based on Marx, answer that and you know where the law will go.

On 31 January 1865, the 13th Amendment was passed by Congress; soon after it was ratified by the requisite number of states. As of 20 June 2021, Juneteenth – marking that date of 19 June 1865 when Texans were informed that slaves were freed – is a Federal Holiday.

For all the *"moral"* arguments, the reality is that slavery is not economically profitable – if you own a slave, you must feed, clothe, house, and provide medical care for that slave. It is a valuable asset that, like a machine, needs to be maintained – only the machine is cheaper to own and operate.

If you're a leader, you realized that Karl Marx emerged in the period when Britain was ending the slave trade. There were other things also happening, and Marx was placing them in an economic context.

So we understand the terms, as used by Marx, here are his definitions.

The proletariat is that class in society which lives entirely from the sale of its labour and does not draw profit from any kind of capital; whose weal and woe, whose life and death, whose sole existence depends on the demand for labour – hence, on the changing state of business, on the vagaries of unbridled competition. The proletariat, or the class of proletarians, is, in a word, the working class of the 19th century.

In our terms, those of the 21st-century, the *"proletariat"* are the lowest class of workers; the *"bourgeois"* of the Marxist era are now what our politicians refer to as the 1-percent.

But, Marx would include the Middle Class whose consists of the leadership class as traditional politicians – the modern nobility.

The 1-percent manipulates the average person – feeding them the delusion what-to-be leaders are somehow different from those they seek to replace. The harsh reality is that they are all of the same genetic stock with ancestral roots whose origins can be traced back to either European nobility or the ancient Hebrews – in many cases, to both.

The most common leadership grabbing technique is to attack your own on behalf of those you seem to control. This is done because you know what you can attack that will resonate with the *"proletariat,"* while not harming your continued status among the *"bourgeois."* The only guidepost is to always focus on the *"big-name individual"* – the Donald Trump of the era.

That means, the technique is to focus attention on those who appear to be wealthy – they must always be the common enemy of those seeking to establish themselves in the ranks of the *"bourgeois."*

Leading up to his election, Donald Trump was a symbol of wealth; when he was elected, the popular propaganda was he lied about his wealth and everything else on his agenda.

As with Marx, we can go back to the Roman era, advance into Shakespearian times, then into the modern era where we see Hitler, and then Joe McCarthy, use the Jew as symbolic of those who have all the money and control everything – they are the segment of leadership to attack.

Curiously, Marx was a Jew and other Jews identified the sound economic logic Marx was building upon. There is a solid basis {found in the Bible} for building an economic foundation that ensures the least among us does not want for basic needs.

Slavery is one way to provide for those needs. But, when people are willing to provide for themselves, the idea of slavery makes no sense – the independent worker is a far better and cheaper slave.

The British, and all of Europe, had a history of peasants and surfs – slaves who provided for themselves while also being subservient to the Noble Lord who was their Master.

In 2021, the terminology has changed but the structural reality continues. Under Biden, the popular rhetoric is to assert racism while practicing it.

Rather than work to improve the base conditions that give rise to future opportunities, we hear *"white supremacy"* – people objecting to the fact that Western cultural advancement originated in Europe rather than Africa.

And, Covid-19 has provided a basis to, once again, turn on the Asian community – the Chinese who are also responsible for many of the things which define modern civilization. After the American "Chinese Exclusion Act" and the British Empire "Opium Wars" attacked China, it abandoned its love of scholars and strong work ethic to be "Communist." It failed.

As defined by Russia and all who oppose Old Testament teaching, Communism must always fail – yet, Democratic America has, as we will see in another chapter, implemented the enumerated ideas presented in the *Communist Manifesto*.

OK, not all the enumerated ideas or goals have been set into play, but Congress is working at it.

The concepts of democracy, republic, or a democratic-republic – as defined in, or interpreted from, the Constitution

– are persistently asserted with varying degrees of success. The fact is, implemented properly, the Constitution can be seen as the forerunner to doctrines put forward by Marx and Engels.

Our leaders know this.

But knowing it, they talk about equality and equity in a way that will ensure the survival of the class structure overseen by a centralized government.

If you want to have true "equality," first recognize that all people are not truly equal – those components of genetics that are invisible make sure of that. Some people are born with strong immune systems, while others are born damaged or with susceptibility to infection. Some are born with a very high intelligence potential, others with fantastic imaginations and talents suited for artistic expression.

The idea that everyone must work, and then defining the work as a mindless routine, means you are imposing inequality on the brilliant and creative whose compelling genus might not be recognized within their lifetime.

Think of Vincent Willem van Gogh. He lived only thirty-seven years and was supported by his younger brother. Yet, here we are, 130-years after his death by suicide, and his name resonates among the premier arts. How many with the talent that would generate a modern van Gogh are being suppressed for lack of a Universal Basic Income?

How many major advancements in modern technology, the arts, and culture have come about because either a parent or sibling had the resources to support the one who created them?

The "*proletariat*" is defined by those who need "equity and Equality" so that the creative intelligence in their families can step forward to advance society. UBI, not some race biased quota, can correct that problem.

We also have the issue of social interaction. We should be encouraging inter-cultural contact and marriage. We know this. It's the whole bit about being *"above your station in life"* or below it.

For social advancement and equality to occur, the cycle must be broken. We know and practice this – it's why we have the idea behind school integration.

Desegregation is impossible. People like to associate and live with those most like themselves.

Those who strive for personal want to advancement, or want their children to advance, will hang out with people better than they are. They pick those associates whose behavior is worth emulating and reject those whose behavior is negative. And by doing so, they will drift in the proper direction. Or, they will hold to their comfort zone and see that their children are in a position associate with those who will advance.

There is another thing that those who want to be leaders or want their children to be leaders, will need to keep in mind. It was neatly stated by the actor Warren Beatty, whose sister is the actress Shirley MacLaine: *"You've achieved success in your field when you don't know whether what you're doing is work or play."*

If a person is forced to work, then they are not engaged in play. Workfare is slavery designed to ensure the individual is among the least productive – that they are locked into that realm or caste defined as the *"proletariat."*

The Silent Generation has been working hard to ensure that the cycles are repeated, that cultural advancement fails. It is also the Silent Generation who are promoting the "Socialist" ideas or pathways which could best serve the current and future centuries or human survival.

CHAPTER Ten - Genetics has a role

Leadership takes many forms. One of the most critical aspects is that of responsibility as encapsulated an expression made famous by President Harry S. Truman: *"The Buck Stops Here."*

Having been placed in charge of handling the Southern Border Crisis created when President Biden took office, it took five months into their administration for Vice President Kamala Harris to finally visit the focus of her responsibility. When she did, she made it a point to steer clear of the crisis 'epicenter.'

In preparation for what she was going to turn into little more than a meaningless photo-opt to silence critics, Harris was reported to have been searching for a way to blame former President Trump for Biden's decisions.

Arriving in El Paso, Texas on 25 June, Harris claimed that it was "*always the plan*" – meaning the fact that Trump had announced his border visit for the following week in no way influenced her actions.

She then told the media: "*We are here today to address, and to talk about what has brought people to the U.S. border, and against continue to address the root causes, cause people to leave their home country. ... The important aspect of this visit is leading this visit after the work that we did in Guatemala and Mexico. It's not a new plan. But the reality of it is that we have to deal with causes, and we have to deal with the effects.*"

Ignoring the history of the Obama-Biden administration, Harris then told the media: "*El Paso being the birthplace of the previous administration's family separation policy. It is an important part of the story here, and one that you can expect we will continue to tell tomorrow on the ground.*"

By assigning responsibility to Harris, Biden will be free to blame her for the outcome of his open border policy, which is contrary to Senator Obama's Secure Fence Act legislation and subsequent Presidential achievement. Biden will use Harris to ensure the "buck" does not reach his desk.

It took only five months of the Biden Administration to undo everything that had been achieved since Reagan's Open border amnesty set the standard for mass illegal crossings and drug smuggling along the Southern Border.

In terms of allowing illegals to enter into the country and creating massive budget deficits on their behalf, and as a result of pandemic-related actions, it only took a few months for Biden to significantly out-Reagan President Ronald Reagan.

Throughout the first six months of his administration, MSM and New York City had joined forces to keep the focus on Trump – New York State even went so far as to temporarily suspend former NYC Mayor and Presidential Counsel Rudy Giuliani right to practice law.

Obviously, when they say *"The Buck Stops Here,"* those who are actively undermining the national interests are making sure the "Here" is the desk of a former administration and not the current one.

It is possible the Biden is not using Harris as a shield, but is simply adhering to the idea of *"leading from behind"* – this is something associated with a modern general and is especially applicable to a Commander in Chief.

In terms of leadership, the Chinese philosopher Lao Tzu is credited with saying: *"To lead people, walk behind them."*

Many people might assert Lao Tzu was wrong – leaders are supposed to lead, they're supposed to be at the forefront. The idea of leading by walking behind is counterintuitive to all who are not true leaders.

In many modern situations, number two is superior to number one. When you walk into a meeting with people you are not familiar with, the smartest person might be the personal assistant to a given individual who is generally perceived to be the leader.

The personal assistant might have more influence over a given outcome than their boss.

Think about it and, if you are a leader, you'll understand and recognize you have seen it more times than you can recall. Phrased one way, "A Leader Serves." To be a leader, there are common instances when, or professions where, you might wish a career as "Number Two" in the "Power Structure" or perceived "Food Chain."

We have all seen this on TV; it is often a basis for comedy in a corporate structure environment. But we also know it from military scenarios – the character of Radar in the series MASH, or SARGENT BILKO.

Many individuals who are natural-born leaders prefer to hide that fact – the WIZARD OF OZ hid behind a curtain and it was from there that he controlled everything. If you go to a shop where you will haggle over a price – a car dealership, or a real estate brokerage firm, are common examples – you will often hear the line, *"I need to check with my manager."*

You might not realize that the salesman is the owner or has full autonomy and authority to close deals. The manager or superior does not exist. But it has a strategic effect to claim that there is one.

We see the same tactic in political semantics. Politicians will use the inclusive "WE" or talk of "bipartisan" legislation when only one or, at most, a handful of the opposition signs on. They are so entrenched in this con that when a rare person like Donald Trump enters their territory they panic.

Trump utilizes somewhat different rhetoric – his name gets stamped on a project, appears on a stimulus check. He will refute things using a vague "people say" or "I was told" when he repeats data he knows to be questionable.

On the other hand, even when he is in the process of taking credit, he praises those who made the success possible.

He elevates those who are loyal to him, and gives them praise for good work; he also destroys those who are incompetent or oppose him. And, because some people take advantage of him, he has projects that fail. As the expression goes, *"That which does not kill me makes me stronger."*

Ever since the 2016 election results were announced, it became clear that MSM and others were devoted to killing off Trump – he was a dangerous transitional outsider.

Keep in mind that, for those seeking to enter politics, politics is a highly competitive environment that is dominated by a network of insiders who repeatedly prove they do not want to move higher. If they have achieved a level of secure power, it is not in their best interest to be elevated to a higher and more complicated or venerable position.

NFL football coach Bill Walsh said he *"observed that if individuals who prevail in a highly competitive environment have any one thing in common besides success, it is failure – and their ability to overcome it."*

Overcoming failure or surviving events that would kill off others is a situation most people try to avoid. But, when we see someone like Donald Trump, we witness what it is like to base your strategy on using failure as a stepping stone to much greater success.

As we have seen, Joe Biden has continually exhibited a far different approach – one that is consistent with the normal political approach of the character presented in the BBC series "I, CLAUDIUS."

The story of the post-crucifixion Christian era Claudius is set within the transitional environment that lead to the rise of Nero. In proper terms, it is the story of *Tiberius Claudius Caesar Augustus Germanicus*, one of the five emperors of the Julio-Claudian dynasty whose occupation of Israel served as the catalyst for the emergence of Jesus, whose alleged followers would eventually conquer Rome and its European empire. That "conquest" would initiate a chronological pattern that defines fulfillment of the Book of Revelation which will be finalized by the Middle eastern initiation of a Third World War in the years surrounding 2033 – twelve years from the writing of this book.

In terms of the analogy, Trump would be Caligula (*Gaius Julius Caesar Augustus Germanicus*), Biden is Claudius, and we have yet to identify the political force that was Nero (*Nero Claudius Caesar Augustus Germanicus*). We do know that, in 54AD, Nero became the last direct descendant of Augustus to rule the Roman Empire.

As shown on the rear cover of Book 8 of the Trump Card series, all the Presidents are descendants of four sisters who lived in 1170; as we saw in *Jonathon's POTUS Cousins,* all the cousin connections have, to some extent, been reinstated and or retained, since 1570.

Going back further, all Presidents and European Nobility exhibit a common leadership ancestry that stems from the Carolingian Dynasty. Going back from there – through Charles Martel – they are direct descendants of the Frankish Roman senator Flavius Afranius Syagrius (350-399).

We have no solid data as to the lineage connecting to various Roman dynasties, but modern DNA studies have shown the Italians have a predominance of the predominance of yDNA R1a, J2, and E3b1. {for the details see: Francesca Brisighelli, 2007, Molecular Phylogenetics and Evolution, *"Y chromosome genetic variation in the Italian peninsula is clinal and supports an admixture model for the Mesolithic–Neolithic encounter."*}

As seen through the yDNA analyses that served as the basis for *GRANDPA WAS A DEITY*, the dominance of R1a1 is consistent with the emergence of the Indo-European culture and is the dominant genetics in both Brahmin and Ashkenazi "tribal or caste" groups. This leadership data is also consistent with the chronological data that was the basis for the twenty-four eras (patriarch ages) explored in GENESIS OF GENESIS.

Leadership runs in family lines. When those lines are broken, the nation being lead falls into hard times or becomes a historical footnote. This brings us to Nero and the POTUS who will replace Biden.

If the analogy is to hold, the next American President, POTUS-47, will conform to the genetic pattern. If the Biblical prophecy pattern is to hold, the 2032 election will see a break in the pattern; since there are eight years between the end of the current Biden term and the 2032 election, the individual who serves as our modern Nero could be a two-term president.

If it was a perfect analogy, Biden could survive a second term; his successor dies near the end of his term – elevating his Vice President into office.

However, like both Mike Pence and Kamala Harris, that individual will not be part of the ancestral line and thus brings an end to the historical continuity that has marked the leading Western nations.

As has been observed among mammals, those assuming leadership are genetically connected to their predecessor.

When we look at the "Lion King," it is their offspring or genetic cousin who ascends to the role of leader of the pride.

As we know, the Bible contains marriage laws that apply to Tribes in the same way to Indian Castes – in both cases, each marries within its own. Ruling over each Tribe or Caste there is a common leadership Caste – the Hebrews had the Levites, with the Kohanim as the religious class; the cultural structure of India has the Brahmin.

The ancient character of the Indus Valley Civilization does not allow for the identification of religious leadership that would equate to the Kohanim, but yDNA shows that Brahmin and Ashkenazi are the same R1a1 and J2. We can assume that, as with the Kohanim, early Indian religious leaders were from the J2. The R1a1 were the invading Aryans who claimed to be the children of the sons of the creator deity – hence the book,

Grandpa Was A Deity, and the common tradition connecting China and the Indo-European civilizations.

In the Biblical, the breeding pattern is codified – each tribe marries within its own and thus protects its heritage; those who are Levites marry Levites, and because they have no right of inheritance in the land, they marry across Tribal borders.

If an exceptional person emerges within the tribe, they get the right to marry into the Levite leadership of their tribe, and their might gain the right to marry outside the tribe.

In modern parlance, individuals can, if worthy, marry above their station, If their children prove worthy, they have the opportunity to marry into true leadership– those who dominate all the tribes or control the religious elements.

We see a variation on this with the pressure to marry within your own ancestry or race. And within that tradition we see people marry within their trade. Of course, it is a matter of proximity – you are more likely to mate with a person who is a part of your daily routine.

The idea of exponential ancestral growth – two parents, four grandparents, eight great grandparents, etc – is nonsense. Any genealogy contains evidence that families stay within a distance equivalent to walking in a straight line for ten to twelve hours. With the introduction of aerial surveillance, it was recognized that populations remain within a twenty-five-mile radius. When there is a population shift that cannot be explained by a natural disaster or development of a commercial venture, it often meant the development of a "secret" military facility.

People are creatures of habit and their leaders conform to that tradition. Because of those traditions, patterns repeat.

The Julio-Claudian dynasty lasted about 95-years. If we hold that the modern equivalent emerged with Franklin Delano Roosevelt – inaugurated on 4 March 1933 – the equivalent time frame ends around the time of the 2028 election.

If our Julio-Claudian dynasty analogy holds, then there is a weakness in the first analysis – Biden serves one term and is then replaced by a modern Nero. Will history declare that he too would *"Fiddle while Rome burns"*? A false assertion that survived as lies do; if so, then Trump could be Nero in 2024.

Nero was only about thirty years old when he died, his successor, Lucius Livius Ocella Sulpicius Galba, ruled for only a year before he too died – at the age of seventy. While he was a member of a noble family, Wikipedia states: *"Galba was not related to any of the emperors of the Julio-Claudian dynasty."*

For our purposes, this would mean that President who takes office in January 2029 will not be seen as a descendant of the 4-sisters. That will mark the end of the American branch of the line of traditional European leadership which still survives in Great Britain but, apparently, nowhere else in Europe.

The start of the Third World War could easily begin with the fall of the American government.

When we look at World War 2, Americans might think in terms of 7 December 1941; Europeans might say 1 September 1939; the real beginning was when Hitler began his move to power in 1931 and followed from Hitler's experience in World War One – when German Nobility came to an end.

As we know, when French Nobility was brought down by their Revolution the effects lasted a decade and gave rise to Napoléon di Bonaparte. After the 2020 election, Democrats called for an end to the Electoral College. It was similar to a call that began in 2016 when Trump defeated Clinton.

However, 2016 saw calls for impeachment before the inauguration and we saw – after Biden was elected and before the inauguration – an attempt at a second Trump impeachment intended to stop Trump from running again in 2024. The idea was Trump should be prevented from repeating an achievement attained once before by Glover Cleveland – two victories and two separate administrations.

Bonaparte was descended from minor Italian nobility – so a pattern of leaders from a leadership class holds, even as the critical line or link was broken. France fell and gave rise to the British Empire – an Empire upon which the sun never set.

Just as Britain replaced, or won over the colonial French Empire, China now seeks to achieve mercantile victory over the United States.

Because Climate Change is expediting the move to renewable energy, the Middle Eastern oil nations – which have not developed any real industries – cannot hope for a place in this pattern of development. In our string of analogies, the Middle East is colonial Germany. The best they can hope for is control over neighboring states – something Muslim nations have been fighting to achieve for the past fourteen hundred years.

As with Hitler's Germany, the anti-Israel Muslim states will be the cause of World War Three – and they will lose.

But, in terms of leadership, for our purposes, our focus must remain on the Julio-Claudian dynasty analogy. Caligula – the third of the five Julio-Claudian dynasty emperors – was, in terms of exhibited hatred, the equivalent of Trump. He was so hated that the Roman Senate tried to erase him from history.

As we know, the greatest publicity and assurance that you will be remembered is to have people hate you. Because they hate you, they cannot stop talking about you. For someone like Donald John Trump, being attacked assures of a solid place in history – it is far superior to having your name on structures that will eventually crumble into dust or be torn down.

Caligula is not the problem. The real problem is Nero.

Nero was one of the most brutal Emperors, he killed at random because he could. Remember Bill Clinton's response when asked why he engaged in his extra-marital practices? He was clear about it – saying, "Because I could."

Biden opened the borders and created the crisis Harris

has avoided addressing – because, with an Executive Order, he could. Similarly, Pelosi and Schumer will work to make things worse – again, because they can, and it serves their interests to create the most long-term harm they can.

Claudius became Emperor by accident. With Biden the call is voter fraud in an election environment that had a record voter response – 150 million votes; 8 million determining the President; the possibility, or reality, of dead voters and illegal voters swaying the outcome in various states.

But it doesn't matter. The election was certified, and the claim of a problem has been classified as "The Big Lie" that is being promoted by Trump and his supporters.

Biden is the President. There is no legal Constitutional structure for reversing an election. And if it was attempted, it would through into doubt any signed legislation or Executive Order effects. In reality, it could initiate an environment where legal chaos would define the nation for decades.

Remember, the rear cover of book eight of the Trump Card series – 2020 IMPEACH V HISTORY – shows the kinship of the 4-sisters; in March 2020, before the formal nomination of Joe Biden, it showed the prediction that a nominated Biden would be POTUS-46.

It was simple, Trump is descended from two of the 4-sisters, and Biden from three. Tulsi Gabbard also shows on the cover – she's a descendant of all four sisters and, therefore, the perfect candidate for any political party that wants a leader who could benefit the nation. But the political parties, or the nation, have no interest in an attractive, intelligent, female President.

If we look to Nancy Pelosi and Elizabeth Warren, we see they routinely provide basic evidence for asserting women are not suited for the type of power that accompanies being the Commander in Chief of the most powerful nation in history.

Because it is the most powerful nation – as with ancient Rome – when the United States falls things will get interesting.

Potential leaders are looking around and observing that the foundation for the destruction has been under construction since the Reagan era. In the current incarnation, we have "*The Big Lie*" – the idea that the election involved fraud.

Trump is the focus, but "*The Big Lie*" began with Hillary Clinton's team. Looking back we find the former Democratic Senate Majority Leader Harry Reid promoting the conspiracy theory about Russia influencing the 2016 election tally.

A related 2020 book by a Washington Post reporter has a quote attributed to Reid: "*I think one reason the elections weren't what they should have been was because the Russians manipulated the votes. It's that simple. It doesn't take a math expert to understand that by changing a few votes, the outcome will be different. So, I have no doubt.*"

On 13 July 2018, a District of Columbia grand jury went so far as to indict 12 Russian military intelligence officers who allegedly interfered with the 2016 election. But where did the investigation by former FBI chief Robert Mueller go – what was the result?

There was a report on the findings which found there was no evidence of collusion or conspiracy involving either Trump or Russia. However, since it was an attack on Trump, it avoided any wording that would exonerate Trump.

"*The Big Lie*" being promoted by the Clinton Democrats did achieve something. It began a mental degradation process that allowed Trump to turn the tables and accuse Democrats of manipulating events to elect Biden. This claim of fraud was strengthened by the record number of votes received by Trump, and the narrow margin by which Biden won.

Of course, the Muller investigation is forgotten and there is a continuous focus on Trump as the creator of "*The Big Lie.*" The beauty of the process is that "*The Big Lie*" can be a lie that serves a purpose – in numbs the brain of the average citizen so that when real fraud is attempted, it is not believed and facts are not disclosed because there is no investigation.

While the numbing process is underway, the leaders who sponsored the lie are in the process of weakening the election system – no need for voter ID or any proof of legal eligibility to vote. Any effort to examine voter registration rolls for those who might have moved or died is opposed – it's even painted as an effort to manipulate subsequent elections.

Hillary Clinton is not a descendant of the 4-sisters; her only claim to the leadership position is through her marriage to Bill Clinton – who is descended from the same three sisters as Joe Biden.

Neither Trump nor Clinton gain from an extended brain-numbing, conspiracy theory, exercise – they are too old. If the conspiracy theory can be invoked in 2024, the benefits will fall to those who run in 2028 or 2032.

If the current Congress undermines the process, there is the possibility of real fraud occurring in the 2022 election. But there need be no actual fraud or interference. There only needs to be an implanting of subliminal doubts and fears of the type that accompanies leaders denying the need to apply basics to the process.

We need ID or proof of age to buy tobacco products and alcohol; we need driver's licenses; we are give given a card to prove we have had a Covid-19 vaccination – yet we do not need one for smallpox, polio, the flu, any other vaccination against infectious disease.

Of the examples, voting seems to match the vaccinations – do we need a card or not? Comically, the call for voter ID is highest where availability and a willingness to have the Covid-19 vaccine are the lowest.

But with both – if not, why not?

As published since the beginning of the pandemic, Covid-19 is a culling virus – it only kills those who would likely have died from a pre-existing condition within a year. The problem is that, as more people are vaccinated, the virus will seek other hosts – killing any who have an unrecognized medical issue.

But, because this is a book and not a news story, the act of accepting or rejecting the free vaccine is academic; as such, it is for leaders to use to prepare for the next – undoubtedly far worse – a pandemic that will emerge as a byproduct of climate change. HIV and Monkeypox exposed the pattern.

The voting issue is different. Voting by mail allows many opportunities for mass-produced fraud – election officials have no idea who filled out or mailed in the ballot. There is also a second layer where the votes mailed in do not matter – if a malevolent agent wishes to control an election, what better way than to have opposing ballots negated?

How do you void a ballot? Easy, have the person vote twice. The voter votes in person, and their name is recorded. But, unknown to the voter, a malevolent agent had submitted a mail-in ballot with their name on it, and after the polls have closed the second ballot is discovered and both ballots are void.

Of course, electronic voting is subject to manipulation or hacking under conditions where the voter has no idea what was recorded by the machine. The machines are not vaccinated anymore than your computer is – though you do have the option to buy security software {electronic vaccine}.

Computers and AI are quickly becoming an integral part of the leadership gene pool. Figuratively, Artificial Intelligence is likely to replace government leadership – not the elected officials. AI will replace many levels of bureaucrats who exist to create a continuity of policy that spans elected leaders.

On many levels, replacing bureaucrats with AI serves a positive purpose and increases efficiency. But elected officials must want to improve efficiency – but routinely demonstrate they have opposed a government that is both functionally and economically efficient. If they wanted efficiency, they would institute a Universal Basic Income and Universal Health care –

they would also do away with the Graduated Income Tax.

Flat taxes on all income beyond that diverted to generate income are economically sustainable and have proven to be far more efficient.

Universal Basic Income serves a dual purpose. First, it is universal and therefore replaces the personal deductions on tax forms. UBI is untaxed income and also serves to replace the vast majority of welfare-related services. When every citizen is assured they can have a basic livelihood, they are free to work in fields they might reject on economic grounds.

TRUE! Some people would avoid gainful employment – but why complain about it? We seem proud to maintain non-productive workers – isn't that a basic motivation for religious groups? What do Priest, Rabbis, or Mullahs produce? Their homes and places of business are tax-exempt and there is even a tax system for the exemption of secular "charities" or other not-for-profit groups that rank in millions of dollars annually.

Of course, the immediate response is MARXISM! After all, weren't Marx and Engels opposed to religion in a time when there was no Federal Income Tax?

Comical, isn't it? Easily seventy years before ratification of the Sixteenth Amendment, and a full century before there was television and the televangelists who learned they could live in million-dollar mansions without really working or paying taxes, Marx and Engels were denouncing their con-artistry.

Now, in 2021, social media is filled with those pointing out that the richest people pay pennies while average workers pay thousands in annual income and other taxes.

But, again, if you are born into the genetic pool of leadership, the system works for you. As seen in the Biblical marriage laws, good leaders structure the system so qualified individuals rise to the top.   The offspring of the worker class can become leaders through education.

CHAPTER Eleven - MARX & ENGELS

In looking at Marx, it is wise to first examine teachings from the Old Testament and the works of Confucius.

As mentioned, when the rolls of the Twelve Tribes were defined, two tribes were economically intertwined – Zebulun {merchants] and Issachar {scholars}. The Scholars appear to have been the most important and, therefore, were to be fully supported by the merchants.

Without scholars, no society can advance and there is no technology or knowledge for the merchant to utilize. As we know, the northern states quickly created colleges, while the southern ones outlawed education for their workers {slaves}.

About two millennia before Harvard came into existence, and about eight centuries after Moses, the Chinese philosopher Confucius prioritized four basic "occupations." Being a scholar was first, followed by the farmer who provided food for the people, the worker who provided non-farm services, and finally, we have the merchants who, by selling the surplus production, provided a basis for the exchange of services and the products which introduced cash flow and national economic growth.

Merchants do not create, they merely distribute surplus production. By doing so, they bring wealth and variety to the nation. Regional communities with a central marketplace can survive without the merchant class. But, for a nation to exist, it must have commodities to trade. National wealth relies on importing that which can not be domestically produced.

It is not about a balance of trade. Trade deficits are nice doom-and-gloom topics, but not important. The issue is wealth – what benefits are derived from the international trade. Those who doubt that must reconcile the fact that America routinely runs a trade deficit but still manages to be one of the wealthiest nations in history.

Wealth is prosperity for those who have it. For a nation

to be truly wealthy, and hope to survive, the least among them must be secure, must have all their basic needs met. In the Star Trek series, this was achieved by everyone having free access to a replicator – they ask, and they receive that which they need.

In the real world, we are entering an age in which homes can be build using "replicator" technology that was first used to convert a design on paper into a three-dimensional figure.

We are entering the age of Star Trek – an AI-controlled cashless society that Marx could not envision. Marx spoke to the menial worker, the illiterate manual laborer who has been replaced by scholars, merchants, and engineers.

Think about it. Scholars devise a computer application to control an engineer-designed machine that converts a digital image to a physical one; then merchants sell the product. The machines can now plant, care for, and harvest crops – what was manual farm work becomes a human-directed exercise in the use of Artificial Intelligence.

Nations like the United States have emerged to show the importance of international trade merchants, whose skills are augmented by agricultural production. As many know, in the 1960s economists looked at America in terms of traditional economic thinking and declared it a Third World Nation that was dependent upon agriculture for its balance of trade.

But economists were thinking like Confucius and Marx.

In terms of Marx, the only advanced thinking was that he chose to phrase things in terms of "surplus capital" – in terms of what the merchant produces and should use to support the scholars.

In the *Communist Manifesto*, Marx states he is opposed to reducing the average laborer to the level of bare existence as represented by the then minimum wage, *"All that we want to do away with, is the miserable character of this appropriation [used to prolong and reproduce a bare existence], under which the labourer lives merely to increase capital, and is allowed to live only in so far as the interest of the ruling class requires it."*

When Marx was theorizing, the ultimate minimum wage was slavery, which was followed by the pay scale and conditions depicted in the works of Dickens. And neither of those can describe the modern world – thus negating some of the Marxist ideas.

But wage-slavery exists. Consider a minimum wage paid for tip-based employment. It hasn't changed in four decades.

The pandemic closed restaurants and workers realized they could do better – so we hear about people not wanting to work, or demanding better conditions.

Consistent with an approach that sells propaganda-based foolishness, we are told people are not working because the $300/month in extra unemployment insurance has resulted in people making more by staying home than by working.

Comparing income from a 40-hour workweek, or a 160-hour work month, and a change of $300/month, or $1.875 per hour. Think about that Giving someone the equivalent of $1.88 over what they were earning is, according to various political scam artists, enough to get them to sit at home and forego the money they were earning.

People aren't very bright. Or, about a third of any given population is not too bright. However, we routinely see that in the response to various things – including the call for what is a Federal Level or National Community College type free college education.

Remember, as we have noted, from the stated origin of the Biblical Tribes to Confucius, and then through Karl Marx, those whose thinking has been embedded in history have placed the role of a Scholar above all other professions and endeavors.

Without scholars, no nation has ever achieved levels of technological and intellectual advancement, or any significant level of historical continuity. Go back to the beginning of the Bible, the *Book of Genesis,* and what the idiot class refers to as the "Original Sin" – the acquisition of knowledge.

In today's world, those who prize stupidity and ignorance oppose free education through college or university.

Thus the issue is whether such advancement is important or not – do we want to live like Adam before Eve fed him from the Tree, or do you consider the advancement which followed over the next 5781 years to be worth the trouble or being kicked out of the wilderness jungle called "Paradise"?

If you chose "Paradise", be mindful of the fact there are still tribes in India, Africa, and South America, who walk about in loincloths (which, because Adam walked naked, you would discard). They enjoy and experience the "Garden Paradise" – if you're worthy, you are perfectly free to join them.

Of course, those who speak of either an original or future "Paradise" aren't rushing off to live completely naked and alone in the jungle.

Part of "wisdom" is realizing how stupid that would be.

Everything begins with wisdom and scholarship – when we set aside the idea that the deity was too stupid not to know, when he created a serpent that could talk to Eve, events would unfold in a way that brought wisdom to Man – it is clear that the Bible declares Wisdom above Blind Obedience.

The all-wise, all-knowing, Biblical deity wanted man to be able to think, reason, and advance. Alternatively, possibly, that divine entity was a total idiot – one who did not know that, when you command someone to only eat a vegetarian and fruit diet, you do not tell them not to eat a beneficial fruit.

When the entity you created obeys, you certainly do not create a creature who can talk to him; then create a partner or mate who that creature can convince to disobey, because *"The Forbidden Fruit"* will elevate their status.

Consider that it is those who claim to worship an *"all-knowing entity"* who did not know the ramifications that the serpent and female would introduce. They oppose scholarship, many among those who claim to worship a Jew and follow his interpretation of the Jewish teachings were the forerunners of those murdering Jews for following those same teachings – but were worshiping the one Jesus worshiped, rather than Jesus (or doing it through Jesus).

Marx pointed out, *"When the ancient world was in its last throes, the ancient religions were overcome by Christianity. When Christian ideas succumbed in the 18th century to rationalist ideas, feudal society fought its death-battle with the then revolutionary bourgeoisie. The ideas of religious liberty and freedom of conscience, merely gave expression to the sway of free competition within the domain of knowledge."*

It is a historical summary worthy of some discussion.

Marx then talks of the idea of *"eternal truths"* and then says, *"Communism abolishes eternal truths, it abolishes all religion, and all morality, instead of constituting them on a new basis; it therefore acts in contradiction to all past historical experience."*

Is this a negative? The alleged *"eternal truths"* are to be abolished, replaced, and re-established on a new basis that will be seen to contradict *"all past historical experience."*

Is Marx attacking religion and society? Or is he, in 1848, envisioning a beginning to a new world of social interaction and technology which negates traditional ones?

In the 1600s, people believed witchcraft was an *"eternal truth"* and plagues were one manifestation of the *"truth."* And, if not caused by "witches", plagues were the product of demons that their *"all-powerful"* deity could not control, subdue, or in any way eradicate.

Traditionally, there are the *"eternal truths"* that religions view demons and Satanic forces as the means by which the *"all-powerful entity"* forces humanity to worship him. Without such supernatural forces, why would anyone give ten percent of their hard-earned money to support a Priest who does nothing beyond telling them he can remove their sins and exempt them from eternal punishment in an *"afterlife"* life?

The *"afterlife"* life is the "eternal life" presented by the *Tree of Life* – Adam and Eve were kicked out of paradise so they couldn't eat from it. Now we are told we die and receive eternal life – granted, in Heaven or Hell, but still eternal life.

Is it an *"eternal truth"* in which all souls are to remain ignorant – except for the religious *bourgeoisie*?

Marx rejected that idea.

Let us look at *"eternal truth."*

We start with the fact that the core of any community is a "General Store" and school. The General store – the place to buy food, household supplies, and any basic item or tool – is a must-have.

Even in this modern age, where travel is easy and we can traverse in under an hour what once required a full day, nobody wants to get into the car and drive an hour to get a container of milk or bottle of ketchup.

When people say *"convenience store,"* they mean they want something that is convenient access. The *"eternal truth"* is that every level of society relies on access to the basics. If the community loses a local grocery or *"convenience store"* it will die

Mention Welfare or a far more efficient Universal Basic Income, and you are talking about the funds that keep those critical businesses alive.

They are the foundation of every economy – try to find a neighborhood grocery in a "Third World" nation. Or, even better, in that "loin cloth paradise" where people are still living the hunter-gatherer lifestyle.

The *"eternal truth"* that changed, and was in the process of changing in the time of Marx and Dickens, is that agrarian cultures are vanishing. The modern *"eternal truth,"* which the

Marxist concept was attempting to prepare for, is one in which even rural living is "*connected.*" The "*eternal truth*" is a world seen from your easy chair. A world of Zoom, Skype, and other modes of video conferencing or communication that were the future when New York City hosted the 1964 World's Fair.

The new "*eternal truth*" is about products of scholarship and human creativity – the fruits of the Tree of Knowledge are taking root and creating a true forest paradise.

By asserting that Scholars should not be self-supporting, Moses affirmed the reality of the "divine intent." Confucius was showing his affirmation, and when modern politicians call for free university tuition, they are affirming Moses and Confucius.

In a mercantile culture society, UBI is simply declaring the Merchant Class should support Scholars – while everyone benefitting from a reliable basic income rather than a "personal tax deduction."

Karl Marx was theorizing about events that would follow the Industrial revolution which, at the time of his writing, was about eighty years old. Accordingly, he elevated the rank of the worker above that of the farmer, while the merchants continue to foot the cost.

As we will see, America has adopted some elements of Marx and Communism – under both Conservative and Liberal banners – while establishing that the Marxist view of the future is not the one that eventually emerged to be the current era of AI and electronic technology.

The world of Karl Marx was the world of Charles Dickens and child labor, with coal as the modern source of power.

Marx was also writing at a time when photography was new and New England had made use of native hackmatack trees to establish itself as a mercantile ship-building force that would dominate "Tall Ship" based world trade into the 20th-century.

But, that is one view of the era, for another, we have the letters of Frederick Engels in which he describes the economics of his era.

Looking to a letter dated 21 January 1882 – thirty-five years before the Revolution commonly marked as beginning Socialist activity and Communism – Engels tells us: *"in Russia we find, along with the feverishly developing capitalist order, bourgeois ownership in land only in the process of development, while the greater part of the land is held in common by the peasants as community property."*

Socialist community property held by the peasants was already established as an accepted practice in Russia. Though Engels does acknowledge it was *"already a very disintegrated form of primitive communal land ownership, pass over directly to a higher Communist form of land ownership, or must it first undergo the same process of dissolution which manifested itself in the historical development of western Europe."*

If we look at the history of Scandinavia, we see Viking era examples of Socialism and communal ownership. There, it has been practiced as Marx would later describe as Communism – they perfected it to the point where they rank among the top 15 in the UN's Human Development Report, the people have a higher percentage of disposable income, and life expectancies are among the longest in the world.

People in the United States are struggling to reach 80 years of age; Scandinavians reach 83; Hong Kong exceeds 85 with Japan running a close second. As of July 2021, the people of 38 nations can expect to live longer, more productive, lives than the average American citizen. The difference? The other nations lean toward, or practice, a form of democracy that some American Politicians denounce as socialism.

When it comes to Standard of Living, we have the false measure of per capita GDP and taxes. When the Golden Rule is applied, when you and your neighbor receive the same high quality of basic services – and are equally taxed – communal standards have a higher base level or foundation.

We tax heavily to create weapons of mass destruction, or to fund the forced necessary to attempt to change of customs or beliefs of others, we lose.

Consider: if the Palestinians devoted the resources they use to attack Israel to improving their territory, they could have the best housing and cities in the Middle east.

Then, toss in resources needed to compensate for Israel's retaliatory response, and Palestinians could afford the schools and industrial development which would elevate them to levels where they would be admired throughout the world.

And, silly as it seems, Israel would be happy to help them attain that level of recognition. Plus, there is the added benefit that it would see the fulfillment of a Koran-related prophecy.

However, rather than help their neighbor, we see a third of humanity work hard to harm that neighbor. When it comes to responding to the attacks by others, we pressure asserted to demand the respondents pull their punches – rather than take appropriate action to eradicate the problem.

Since World War Two, America has sought to make the threat of Russian competition a problem. In Two World Wars, Russia was considered an Allie. And looking back, Engels said, *"look to Russia. At the time of the 1848-49 Revolution not only the European monarchs, but the European bourgeoisie as well, saw in Russian intervention their only escape from the proletariat, which at that time was first becoming aware of its powers."*

Russia as the salvation of the *European bourgeoisie?*

Isn't that the role it played in both World wars? And, is it possible that it was that role, Hitler was referring to when he expressed fear of Russia and the possibility its form of Socialism would overpower the German form?

On 1 February 1893, Engels wrote to reminded his Italian audience: *"While Italy was ruled by the Austrian Emperor, Germany, though more indirectly yet none the less effectively, had submitted to the yoke of the Czar of all the Russias. As a consequence of March 18, 1848, Italy and Germany were relieved of their humiliation. If from 1848 to 1871 these two great nations were reconstituted, and were, in a manner, able to manage their own affairs, it was, as Karl Marx said, because the men who suppressed the 1848 revolution became, in spite of themselves, the executors of its testamentary will."*

The popular revolution of 1848 was a failure, but it did trigger a wave of immigration to the United States which helped strengthen the Northern Republican opposition to slavery.

In his 1882 letter, Engels had mentioned the economic effect of the migration: *"European emigration has made possible specifically the colossal development of American agriculture and has, as a result of the ensuing competition, shaken large as well as small landed property in Europe at its foundation. At the same time, it has made it possible for the United States to tap its rich industrial resources and that with such energy, and upon such a scale, that in a short time an end must be put to the industrial monopoly of western Europe. And both these circumstances react upon America in a manner that pushes it onward to a revolution. The small and medium-sized landed properties, operated by self-employing farmers, the basis for America's entire political system, are yielding more and more to the competition of giant farms, whereas at the same time a proletariat, growing in numbers, is being developed in the industrial districts in conjunction with a fabulous concentration of capital."*

The impact of the 48ers – those who were aligned with the Marx-Engels social doctrine – served to make America into modern America. And note his projection of events coincides with the current state of agricultural ownership and production: *giant farms, industrial districts,* and *a fabulous concentration of capital* among a handful of individuals who own the various technological platforms or industries which are centered in modern *industrial districts* like Silicon Valley.

However, acknowledging the failure, Engels also asserts the revolution of 1848 served to restore national autonomy and unity and restructured relationships between European nations.

As regards Capitalism, Engels' turn-of-the-century letter asserts: "*The Manifesto fully acknowledges the revolutionary acts that capitalism accomplished in the past. Italy was the first capitalist nation. The close of the feudalistic Middle Ages, which opened the era of modern capitalism, was marked by a colossal figure, the Italian, Dante, who was at one and the same time the last medieval and the first modern poet. Today, as in 1300, a new historical era is unfolding. Will Italy give us another Dante to mark the hour of the birth of this new proletarian era?*"

In America, the period following 1882 was marked by the arrival *en masse* of European immigrants and the *new historical era* that unfolded was one of racism and bigotry toward these "outsiders."

Marking the new era, on 6 May 1882, President Chester A. Arthur signed the Chinese Exclusion Act – Chinese labor had built the railroads, they proved they had a strong work ethic – so it was natural for the nation to reject them. Productivity is not something that is to be rewarded and encouraged – at least not if the Workers aren't good Christians.

But, even when they were, as a result of the immigration that accompanied the Irish Potato Famine of 1845 to 1852, NINA – No Irish Need Apply – had been the guiding rule. At least it was until the early 1870s when the railroads expanded westward and the Irish were laying track.

Chinese crews laid ten miles of track over mountains for every mile a comparable size Irish crew could lay over flat land. Immediately it became obvious there must be a Federal law against admitting efficient workers.

With the influx of Eastern European immigrants, there was again a need for immigration laws. Eastern Europeans were mostly Jewish – not a problem. This was the age of the IQ test – the first one having been developed in 1904 by French psychologist Alfred Binet. Twelve years later, after Stanford University psychologist Lewis Terman standardized the original test for American participants, it showed the Jewish immigrants were idiots who offered no promise of productivity.

However, some of their children were exposing the test's fallibility – they were proving qualified for acceptance into the Ivy League Universities. Their academic credentials were such that Harvard went through a period of anti-Semitic enrollment policies – the Jews were out-competing everyone else.

Subsequent IQ testing established that, while the parents and young immigrants could be considered idiots, those born as first-generation Americans scored slightly above normal, or in the genus category. Thus, Anti-Semitism was the order of the day – East European exclusion was reflected in the writing of immigration laws and policies that, prior to the United States entering the Second World War, saw refugees escaping the Nazis being turned away from American ports.

Karl Marx was Jewish. So why listen to him? Or should we say, why acknowledge he was being listened to?

Many structural changes mentioned in the *Manifesto*, have already happened within the United States. For now, we can ignore and focus on the ten things he enumerated. Many readers will recognize them.

1. Abolition of property in land and application of all rents of land to public purposes.

2. A heavy progressive or graduated income tax.

3. Abolition of all rights of inheritance.

4. Confiscation of the property of all emigrants and rebels.

5. Centralization of credit in the hands of the state, by means of a national bank with State capital and an exclusive monopoly.

6. Centralization of the means of communication and transport in the hands of the State.

7. Extension of factories and instruments of production owned by the State; the bringing into cultivation of waste-lands, and the improvement of the soil generally in accordance with a common plan.

8. Equal liability of all to work. Establishment of industrial armies, especially for agriculture.

9. Combination of agriculture with manufacturing industries: gradual abolition of all the distinction between town and country, by a more equable distribution of the population over the country.

10. Free education for all children in public schools. Abolition of children's factory labour in its present form. Combination of education with industrial production, &c., &c...

The first item could be taken to fall under the concept of Federal Land where the government collects money for oil, gas, and other mineral rights. Since rent is paid to use or access, even the "Parl Fees" would be covered.

Then we have the Progressive Income tax which is said to have been introduced by British Prime Minister William Pitt in December 1798. This was further codified as the Income Tax Act 1842.

The United States Constitution had a Property Tax, not an Income Tax; therefore, our tax system does not predate the Communist Manifesto. That said, Abraham Lincoln introduced the first American progressive income tax as the Revenue Act of 1862 – the year before that, the income tax was a flat 3% tax.

As previously mentioned, the Constitutional Amendment in 1913 removed the issues related to taxes on income. After that, it became a matter of manipulating the tax law to exclude the *bourgeoisie* and *clerical nobility* {religious leaders].

If were to check the 2021 speeches by Elizabeth Warren

and others of that ilk, we would see they are advocating attacks on wealth and inheritance.

We can skip property *confiscation* – it exists in multiple forms too numerous or convoluted to enumerate.

Credit? In the emerging cashless society, where only the Federal Government can create money and the Federal Reserve manipulates interest rates, we could say five is accounted for. But, Biden included it in his Infrastructure Bill.

Six centralizes communication – the use of airwaves – and with the creation of Amtrak, railroads were nationalized; as for automotive transport, you need a license, registration, and have strict laws to follow. It would seem the Government does control transportation.

Seven, land use, appears to be a given which, again, has too many examples.

But what about *"Equal liability of all to work"*? Would that conform to the Reagan idea of "Workfare" – if you're on welfare, you need to work? Doesn't matter if that work is both unpaid and serves the business interest of a *"clerical nobility."*

Nine is interesting – and was mentioned earlier in the context of working from home, the internet, climate change, or we could add the Biden open-border immigration policies.

If we accept, as will eventually be necessitated by climate change, those fleeing north from the tropical regions will soon be made uninhabitable by the rise in temperatures. If we do that, we will need to settle them somewhere. Decreasing rural populations, and communities with underutilized schools, have created an ideal resettlement opportunity.

The only problem is political – an *equable distribution of the population over the country* means Congressional and Electoral College representation will equalize.

Ten is a given. Scholars should be the priority.

CHAPTER Twelve - Political Genetics

As we saw with the enumerated Communist goals, there can be no doubt that the United States conforms to all the basic markers for a Communist Country. If we compare the level of United States compliance to that of those regimes which self-identify as Communist, they pale in comparison.

The only real differences are found in America's failure to provide free higher education. We cannot consider medical care, because it is not specifically mentioned by Marx or Engels.

As we know, American history includes bigotry, racism, and early use of germ warfare – in the form of smallpox infected blankets given to indigenous tribes – in the context of Marxist item four, *"Confiscation of the property"*. The latter being done again with the "Trail of Tears" relocation of indigenous peoples from Georgia, Alabama, and Tennessee in 1838.

"Confiscation of the property" from African Americans served as the basis for the creation of New York's Central Park. Again, there is no shortage of examples related to *Confiscation of property* based upon the race of the owner/occupants.

There is also the preemptive *"Confiscation"* represented by segregation and the "Red Lining" process – zoning laws and banking or mortgage practices designed to exclude members of racial and ethnic groups from a given neighborhood.

As with most things in life, we can identify activities that are a mirror image of "Red Lining" – self-congregation.

When African-Americans are excluded from designated "White" neighborhoods, it is deemed wrong. However, when was the last time anyone objected to there being a "Chinatown," "Little Italy," or the "Hasidic" neighborhoods common to New York City.

We do not find it objectionable to designate an area of a community in terms of its predominant religion and respective houses of worship. A house of worship or congregation being central to religion, members of the group will dominate the nearby residences. The same will be seen when a culture or ethnic group is closely related to their food, clothing, or some other traditional commonality.

When we look to those who seek to become the leaders representing those communities, we see them adopt patterns of behavior and speech that resonate with the community. It is the job of a would-be leader to identify with their followers – or at least provide a basis for the herd to identify with them.

If the job is done too well, and the leader is not a part of the dominant political class, power brokers will strive to have the outsider arrested or otherwise silenced. This is a historical pattern commonly seen when a Fascist, dictatorial, or bigoted government runs afoul of an influential leader – their response is imprisonment or execution by assassination.

If we want an example with a positive outcome, we have only to look at South Africa and Nelson Mandela, who served 27 years in prison; then, 4 years after his release, he became the 1st President of South Africa.

On the other end of the spectrum, we have a collapse of Nobility. While we ignore the reality, the United States saw a rebellion of the Nobility against their ruling Nobility cousins.

We've heard the expression about children within a royal family– they need "an heir and a spare." There is a need for a child to inherit the thrown or castle domain, and a second child who would inherit if something happened to the first.

What is generally ignored is the fact that leaders are part of a genetic line, and America's leaders have all been "the spare" or children of that "spare." In 2021, MSM became engrossed in the issue of covered the "problem" of there was the issue of whether or not the children of Harry and Megan can receive the title Prince or Princess.

Those who settled in the colonies and became leaders, or the ancestors of the Revolutionary leaders, were removed from the titles. But they were not so far removed that it was beyond the realm of possibility they would inherit a title – thus we see this reality reflected in Article I, Section 9, Paragraph 8 of the Constitution {Emoluments Clause}. It was also Article VI of the Articles of Confederation.

It wasn't about a fear of bribery.

Rather, it was a recognition that a probable President of the United States could be placed in a position of having a dual allegiance because of his ancestry and various rules governing peerage inheritance, or elevation to a parallel title.

How pervasive is the line? If you can think of someone whose name seems "timeless" – someone born after the colonial settlement of Virginia or the arrival of the Mayflower – and they are probably either Jewish or a descendant of the 4-sisters who were descendants of Charles Martel and Charlemagne.

Think about the media coverage of Harry and Megan vis-a-vis Harry's siblings. OK... the media can focus on Meghan as half-Black, part Jewish, with an unmentioned third heritage. MSM and Social Media place their focus on or emphasize, the black. Sir Arthur John Allen (1520-1572) and other common ancestors are never mentioned.

Why single out Sir Allen?

Maybe because he is also the 12th Great Grandfather of singer and actress Miley Ray Cyrus – who is also a descendant of the 4-sisters and therefore a cousin to all the Presidents.

Significantly, for Miley, that includes Martin Van Buren, Miley's 1st cousin 7 times removed. However, because we lack his genealogical data before the 1500s, Van Buren is the only President we cannot connect to the 4-Sisters.

As we entered the 20th-century, the common connection between the leaders of America and all the European nations was coming to an end – the Nobility was being eliminated from their leadership roles and their nations fell from importance.

One of the last great events related to the influence of the traditional nobility was a fight between cousins that we know as World War One. And this war gave rise to our second example of the entrenched governmental response to any opposition or attempt to overthrow the government.

On 8 November 1923, at an event known as the Beer Hall Putsch, Adolph Hitler was identified as the leader of the Nazis Party's 2000-person protest against the Weimar Republic. The Weimar Republic was incompetent ruling regime that came to power after Germany's World war One surrendered.

For the German people, this was a period of anger over having been forced into accepting the terms of the Treaty of Versailles, which were devastating to the German nation.

As a result of the demonstration, Hitler was arrested; his trial lasted 24-days with full media coverage of a type that made him a national hero. The charge against him was treason, and he received a five-year sentence.

Think about that, five years for treason – a crime which might normally carry a death sentence, and should certainly involve a sentence measured in decades.

On 30 June 2021, comedian Bill Crosby was released from prison after three years of a maximum ten-year sentence for allegedly drugging and sexually assaulting a former Temple University employee in 2004. Interestingly, the prosecutor had granted Cosby immunity from prosecution if he would testify in an unrelated matter – then, without any real evidence, charged him under conditions that violated his 5th Amendment rights.

From what we know, when Hitler was imprisoned he was rather comfortable.

As described by Ernst Hanfstaengl, who visited Hitler in prison, the cell was as if you *"walked into a delicatessen. There was fruit and there were flowers, wine and other alcoholic beverages, ham, sausage, cake, boxes of chocolates and much more."*

It was during this "forced vacation" that Hitler wrote the

two-volume, somewhat biographical, but highly political, *"Mien Kampf."* With all the publicity he had received, the publican in 1925 made him a millionaire. The book was translated and went global as an international bestseller just as the American Stock Market was about to crash. With the events of 1929, the global economy fell, reinforcing the book's assertions about the malevolent agents manipulating the economy.

As with Mandela, upon being released from prison Hitler moved into a position of power. In 1931, capitalizing on *"Mein Kampf's"* success, Hitler moved into government. In 1933, he had a position of power and from there, as the saying goes, the rest is history. Between 1931 and 1945, the global balance of power and influence shifted, and then came the Cold War era.

There was another change brought about by Hitler. The success of *"Mein Kampf"*, combined with the clear evidence of its influence on Hitler's rise to power, lead to a pattern of those with presidential aspirations publishing biographical political tomes.

To date, only seven presidents have written books, and only six were written running and being elected.

1. George Washington wrote one, but, it was published 89 years after his death, so can be disregarded.

2. Theodore Roosevelt described his Spanish-American War experiences in *The Rough Riders* (1899); since he had already established his academic credentials as a historian with the book *The Naval War of 1812* (1882), it was natural for him to record the first-hand account of his recent military experience. He became President because he was vice president when William McKinley was assassinated.

3. John F. Kennedy, *Profiles in Courage* (1954), is the President to write a book because he intended to hold office. The family idea or goal had been for JFK's elder brother, Joseph P. Kennedy Jr., to be the first Catholic

President. But Joe was killed in August 1944, leaving JFK as "the spare" who would achieve the goal.

4. James Earl "Jimmy" Carter, in 1975, created his own autobiographical pre-election campaign advertisement, with the book, "*Why Not the Best?*" – Jimmy Carter was elected in 1976.

5. Barack H. Obama launched his post-Harvard Law political career, in 1995, with *Dreams from My Father: A Story of Race and Inheritance.* He became an Illinois States Senator in 1997, a U.S. Senator in 2005, and President in 2009.

6. Donald John Trump has been utilizing biographical books as a means of self-promotion since 1990. But he is best known for his 2009 book, "*Trump: The Art of the Deal.*" Trump's focus is business, and the stress he responds to with persistence, as touched upon in his 2008 book, "*Trump Never Give Up: How I Turned My Biggest Challenge into SUCCESS.*" We see in Trump an apolitical creature whose approach to business and life has proved perfectly suitable for the political arena.

7. Joseph R. 'Joe' Biden Jr. has published two books – the first, in 2007, preceded his becoming a candidate as Obama's Vice President, and a second published as Trump was completing his first year as President. The first book is the political biography that places Biden's career in some kind of perspective about "*Promises to Keep.*" His second book deals with his son Beau dying of brain cancer – "*Promise Me, Dad: A Year of Hope, Hardship, and Purpose*" – and again he is reflecting on emotional events or and related commitments.

Hitler demonstrated how it was done, and after the war five Presidents utilize "biographies' as a means of eliciting the proper emotional response among the target demographic for achieving a strong segment of that population as their political base.

Of those five presidents, we see only Donald John Trump as one who routinely utilizes Hitler's basic technique to both identify a common enemy and promote his personal image. In the process, he lifts his readers {supporters} by introducing the "self-help" genre into the self-promotion process. Again, this is something an intelligent leader would discern by reading "*Mein Kampf.*"

We need to recognize that, in 1990 – when he published his first biography – Trump told an interviewer that he owned a copy of "*Mein Kampf,*" but would never read the speeches.

At the time, his wife Ivana state he also owned a copy of "*My New Order*" – a compilation of those speeches that had been published on 22 August 1941, about months before *Pearl Harbor.*

Any potential propaganda value to be derived from the publication was therefore disrupted and brought to an end by the Japanese attack. Because it altered history, the Japanese action was extremely significant. In emphasis of that point, keep in mind that, without United States intervention, Hitler should have been able to invade England and win the war.

In a speech given on 30 January 1940, Hitler stated "*The year 1941 will be, I am convinced, the historical year of a great European New Order!*"

But he did not envision that the war in China would see a Japanese miscalculation – the United States had a significant population that agreed with Hitler and had Japan focused on Asia, things might have been considerably different by the end of 1942.

FDR was, like Trump and now Biden, placed in a state of conflict between political extremes. Pearl Harbor disrupted the logical outcome of events in Europe – it forced the Americans to set aside their bigotry and unify behind the flag. "America First" would then become the dominant 20th-century theme; it, like many issues of the period, would then carry forward into the current era of social disruption and change.

Hitler is a model for modern political change or taking key demographic control from a dominant political structure. Reading and analyzing Hitler's writings – including speeches – is far easier than attempting to discern the similar tactics and approaches which are apparent in the Old Testament creation of the Jewish people.

When individuals speak of the Bible, there is a common omission of the idea that Moses was a member of the deposed Hyksos – Shepherd Kings – who had arrived from the territory that is now Palestine, Israel, and Syria. Instead of personal biography, the writers of Genesis created a cultural history that fit both the existing knowledge base and cultural mythology.

This is what traditional leaders do when they conqueror or absorb new territories and peoples. As we were told about the entry into "the promised land" and historians identified among numerous subdued peoples, the first act of the invader is to kill those who might carry on the old traditions.

As mentioned, the colonial era invaders did this through the introduction of decimating diseases.

Climate Change has created a situation where people are forced to invade both Europe and North America. They will also be moving into the once empty territories of Russia, where they will find abundant agricultural resources emerging from the once frozen tundra.

Climate Change means there is a looming choice between defending borders or being an invaded nation. Either way, *The Communist Manifesto* proposed that populations should be spread as evenly as possible throughout the nation.

All citizens oover the age of eighteen should be given the right to vote, and an income sufficient to meet their basic needs for food, clothing, and shelter.

Every individual who is on the path to citizenship – be it a fetus or legal immigrant – should receive regular healthcare.

As the Coronavirus pandemic showed, the health of any given individual can affect the health and ability to remain alive of a stranger, friend, or a member of their family.

As shown in the last two books of the Trump Card series, the Covid-19 virus and all its variants are culling viruses – they only kill those who already had medical issues.

Granted, in a few cases the medical issues had yet to be identified and thus are not cited in the death certificate record, but that does not alter the statistical reality. What it does do is expose the fact that the healthcare system is designed to allow people to die.

We can point to high death counts in other countries, but we must also recognize the extreme longevity enjoyed by their citizens and the fact that, in many cases, it has been artificially maintained – when exposed to the virus, those individuals died.

Then there are places like India, where the population is now being affected – even as virus-connected death counts are falling in European nations. In Idea, there exist numerous demographics, once identified as castes, whose bodies routinely experience "medical" stress. Under normal circumstances, they can adapt to a transient stressor. But when exposed to a Covid variant their immune systems become compromised and death rates increase.

For those who accept prophecy, are superstitious, or are of that ilk who believe in demons and an incompetent creator deity, statistical reality, and classical patterns are ignored. But, that does not alter fact – over the next two or three decades, the number of deaths will remain relatively high and constant. This will not be altered by the fact that we are in a period marked by a global *Baby-Bust*.

Depending on how various forces interact, with nearly 8 billion people on the planet in July 2021, by July 2045, the total should be reduced to about 5.5 Billion. When religious types look back at the peak population, they will proclaim the Book of

Revelation's accuracy and have clear evidence the population of all life had decreased by a third. Over the three decades from 2022 to 2052, national leaders will be dancing to the tune that is defined by changes in demographics and customs.

The question for you becomes one of are you a leader or a member of the anti-leadership Cancel Culture?

Every individual is a leader. Some are like 15-year-old Swedish environmental activist Greta Thunberg, and others are, as we will see, like 19-year-old Gavrilo Princip.

Overtly or covertly, leaders introduce change that alters society. Some achieve this by simply keep the wheels turning – and perform unrecognized critical *"Butterfly Effect"* actions.

Some seek to be the "Lion King" or "Lead Stallion." But, as any naturalist knows, that is a role generally restricted to genetic heritage and upbringing. It also requires planning and a desire to conform to the expectations of the pride or herd.

Among those who aspire to be national leaders, we see those who are selfishly Counter-Culture; they tear up a speech because they want the speaker to be seen negatively as a Hitler-type.

If we again reference Hitler's 1940 speech, something about it resonates in current events:

"In 1918, they declared a blessed and pious age to come! What came to pass in its stead we all lived to see: the old states were destroyed without even as much as asking their citizenry. Historic, ancient structures were severed, not only state bodies but grown economic structures as well, without anything better to take their place. In total disregard of the principle of the right to self-determination of the peoples, the European peoples were hacked to pieces, torn apart. Great states were dissolved."

Even though Hitler wanted to bring down the traditional government of Germany, when the effect was universal – might even call an extension of the Marist view and the Revolution of

1848 – Hitler and his demographic found the way it happened to be very disturbing. They had lost the freedom they desired.

Now rephrase it as 2021 instead of 1918 and think of the states as the existing fifty States. Then think about the Counter-Culture in the context of *"Historic, ancient structures were severed, not only state bodies but grown economic structures as well."* Is there a similarity to be seen of derived?

Two thoughts: The first being: *"Everything is the same, they just change the name or order of magnitude."* And the second: *"Those who are ignorant of history are doomed to repeat it."* And a critical question: *"Are you sufficient a leader to understand the reality?"*

Even if you do not immediately understand, is the person you have chosen to be your leader the person who understands and uses that understanding to better your situation?

Prior to Trump, Conservative voters routinely supported those who would hurt them – those advocating the most harm to the most people policies.

"Law and Order" was not about promoting any form of lawful behavior, it was aimed at either attacking minorities or imposing the will of a minority on the majority. We saw the effect when bigoted idiots asserted the need for "Prohibition"; when that failed to achieve the stated goal; when, as is common whenever you tell people "don't do something that gives you comfort" their instinctive response is to do the opposite, those same idiotic bigots attacked marijuana.

Those seeking power know the reality. They know, when you say no to something that is traditionally acceptable, vast numbers will rebel and provide a visible target. If you can find some statistical reality to point to, something that gets heads nodding in agreement, it becomes easier to make your sale.

Grabbing power is basic salesmanship. You need to get the perspective "buyer" to nod their head before you present the product or objective you seek. Hitler achieved this through the classic focus on the Jewish people. In 1939, Hitler's nephew claimed Hitler's grandmother, was Jewish.

But, a Jew killing Jews? It was a perversely interesting idea of Biblical proportions – a Serpent in a Tree of Knowledge.

If Hitler represented the Horseman of War, and Zionists represented the predicted reestablishment of Israel, then one hundred and forty-four thousand of all the tribes of the children of Israel were destined to die in full view of the world.

Again, to toss a crumb to the religious-right, Revelation 12:6, specifies that a woman would flee into the wilderness for a thousand two hundred and sixty days – about 3 years and 5.4 months. World War Two ended on 8 May 1945, so her journey would have started in December 1941.

The Holocaust would seem to provide perfect cover for the vanishing of 144 thousand Jewish people from all the tribes. And that tosses another crumb to those *"End of Times"* types.

But it would also make Hitler an agent of their boss. And on that score, If Hitler's body had survived, the emergence of yDNA studies would have made it possible to determine his ethnic history.

Lacking a primary source, researchers tested his male relatives – a nephew abandoned Germany and fought against his uncle as part of the American forces, testing that line proved interesting. Their Hitler yDNA showed them to be E1b1 – the very same group that Albert Einstein belongs to.

Einstein was born relatively close to where Hitler had been born, and in the same region dominated by Ashkenazi. It is an interesting and quite explainable crossbreeding reality. It is also interesting that the Haplogroup is North African – there is ample research to say East African Egyptian – and that would infer it could date to the Exodus population. The rumors could have been true.

Why divert into Right-wing Christian issues? What has that got to do with leadership?

Look at who Trump panders to – and how it differs from the more traditional pandering of those who would lead those identifying as Conservative Christian Republicans.

Someone seeking their support might take the presented viewpoint data, twist it slightly so it conforms to their normal rhetorical pattern, and present themself as the leader taking America into the promised new era.

In the vernacular Right-wing Christians subconsciously accept, that candidate would become an agent of their deity fulfilling the *"End of Times"* promise associated 1 Corinthians 13:9: *"where there are prophecies, they will cease; where there are tongues, they will be restrained; where there is knowledge, it will be dismissed. 9 For we know in part and we prophesy in part, 10 but when the perfect comes, the partial passes away."*

The modern rhetoric revolves around lies – who is telling them and do they matter?

People don't want partial truth, they want truth. But, as Marx recognized, Religious groups are based on promoting the same distortions, fantasy, and lies that mark traditional means of population control.

The 1969 *"Summer of Soul"* brought into focus many of the basic issues that are still a part of the rhetoric among those seeking the Black vote. Those same issues resonate with the Hippy turned Conservative Baby-Boomers – those born early in the first decade of the Baby-Boom.

Fifty-two years later, the rhetoric is still focused on the need to vote and voter-rights against a background of exclusion.

Leaders understand things can take time. Change can be made incrementally, or by decisive action. The various Marx-Engels writings made it clear that they understood this – in a context where they were outlining the issues that future leaders would need to address.

Of course, as with religious doctrines, political ideas are either ignored or distorted. If the idea is solid, it will persist and grow a following.

Four hundred years ago, when Britain was fighting over issues of Catholic versus Protestant, it was beginning the fight over the form of leadership that was relevant to the changing times. With the escape to the New World, we see the first move to escape the idea of hereditary rulers.

As seen through animal studies or in Jonathon's POTUS Cousins and subsequent identification of a common leadership ancestry, most recently seen in the 4-Sisters connection, but one that dates back to Charlemagne and his ancestor Charles Martel, and possibly even to a segment of Roman aristocracy – all creatures were designed to have a hereditary leadership.

The difference between Nobility and Reality is found in the difference between *"accident of birth"* order and *"trial by combat."* The system that was brought down by the American Revolution kept the Nobility in power; the French Revolution removed them from power.

However, before either happened, in 1688, the Glorious Revolution initiated a Constitutional Monarchy in Britain – this both retained and removed the hereditary leader by retaining the Crown while also having hereditary and electoral leaders in its two Parliamentary Houses.

The British House of Commons is the American House of Representatives; the American Senate is a variation on the House of Lords. While the US Senate lacks the legal hereditary element of the House of Lords, both the Senate and House have characteristics of multi-generational lifetime employment.

CHAPTER Thirteen - Out-Group

What is an "out-group" and what is a leader?

I've mentioned the Biblical marriage laws. They are an example of a leader legitimizing a normal human activity. The activity is one known as "*Endogamy*" – the practice of marrying within ones' own caste, tribe, religion, ethnic or social group.

"*Endogamy*" is a form segregation that achieves a basic form of apartheid – self-imposed by the minority or out-group. Biblically, it served to maintain the out-group "inheritance."

As with Biblical marriage, researches have observed that the attainment of education or wealth triggers an individual's desire to change groups – to abandon their intimate connection to the out-group and join the Levite "tribe," the *bourgeoisie*.

By suggesting the distribution of the population evenly, Marx sought to neutralized endogamy.

We've taken a brief evolutionary journey through what has become the pattern by which modern leaders have emerged. But, when we focus on government and politics, we address only one role – but is it even a role that holds significance over time?

Think of the world leaders that come to mind. Aren't they all people associated with war? And don't they outnumber those who preached peace?

Look at the Chess pieces depicted on the cover, which one is the "leader"?

We know thc King is the target – Checkmate is the goal of the game, and that means trapping the king where the next move will take {kill} it.

But is the king the actual leader?

Imagine the game played with more realistic rules – ones where, when the king is killed the game continues until one side either loses all its pieces or they cannot move. Play Chess with a Checkers variation.

Each piece has some level of power related to the way it is permitted to move. The female, the Queen, can move in any direction and as far as it can go without jumping over another piece. The knight must move in an "L" – two forwards and one over – but that means it can jump over pieces.

But, then there is the lowly Pawn who, after its first move of one or two spaces forward, can only move forward one space at a time and can only kill a piece diagonally in front of it.

But a pawn also has what no other piece enjoys – it has transformation powers. If it survives to reach the opposite side of the board, it can become any other piece.

Curiously, being a pawn is generally taken to mean you are used by someone else for their advantage. While the idea is consistent with a Chess Pawn, the terminology ignores the idea that the pawn can garner enormous power – if it can traverse the six-box distance to the initial resting place of the opposing nobility.

Any Pawn can be a Castle, Bishop, Knight, or Queen – it can be a leader and command a role in the final victory.

Granted, it cannot become King. But why would it want to surrender chosen mobility for a variation on the one-square move restriction it began with? And why would it wish to be a primary target?

LEADERSHIP requires intelligence.

Many of the most intelligent decide the restrictions on movement and dangers are not worth the title.

In the real world, we have those who are failures – cheats like Biden who resigned from one attempt to become President because it was revealed he cheated, plagiarized when he was in Law School. Because the MSM deems such news to be old news when they are focused on a meatier target, it lost its relevance in the 2020 election.

Besides, the goal was to frame Trump as a cheat – the

last thing that was needed was to present facts of dishonestly Biden had admitted to when he withdrew from the previous election.

In the real world, there are people like Trump who want their name to resonate through history. They seemingly come from nowhere to become THE Leader – and they are attacked.

More importantly, when a group feels threatened, their attacks do not stop.

The New York City political system feels has shown that it is extremely threatened. Schumer, AOC, and the rest know that they represent a modern Tammany Hall that is a disgrace to those of us wishing to remain proud of a life-long Democratic affiliation.

As we move forward, it is becoming harder for the Party to conceal the gross incompetence and dishonesty associated with New York Mayor De Blasio and Governor Cuomo; on the other side of the nation, we have Pelosi and the California recall vote of Governor Gavin Newsom scheduled for 14 September 2021 – after the publican of this book.

All through the Trump administration, we heard calls for his Tax Returns. Finally, New York City was able to obtain them and diverted millions of dollars to their analysis at a time when the City was the epicenter of the Coronavirus pandemic.

But, as expected, since the tax forms have been subjected to routine audits by IRS experts, City prosecutors could find nothing with which to charge Trump.

However, being as corrupt as the rest of modern Tammy Hall Democrats, they decided to file fifteen tax-related charges against the Trump Organization Chief Financial Officer.

Interestingly, they accused Weisselberg and the Trump company of documenting – in filed accounting detail – their 15-year practice of defrauding tax authorities while compensating certain beneficiaries at the company, including Weisselberg himself.

The criminal filing carries with it a subtext proclaiming gross incompetence on the part of all City, State, and Federal tax auditors who might have reviewed the records over the time in question. The firms booked all the expenses and filed them with the Federal IRS and State tax authorities – who approved the deductions, either by not deeming them worthy of an audit or by an audit which found them lawful.

Having been raised as the son of a partner in a major New York City Law firm, and having subsequently gained my own recognition in Who's Who in Finance by running a major national Real Estate operation based in mid-town Manhattan, I could be wrong about motives driving Manhattan District Attorney Cyrus Vance Jr and Attorney General Letitia James.

But having also been an Accounting Specialist for one University and then a Professor of Business Studies specializing in studies for a State University – I doubt I'm wrong.

Of course, if there is a conviction on most or all charges and that conviction stands up to the inevitable appeals, it would eventually appear that I'm mistaken. But, based on the various ramifications which could emerge from the charges, I doubt it will come to that.

The basic claim appears to be the assertion that, instead of the company paying taxes on the reported income used for the benefits given to the executives, the individuals should have.

But the money is only taxable to the individuals, and so each and every person receiving the benefit – which is being called undeclared income – has defrauded the tax authorities, not the Trump Organization.

The records showed, the firm made no effort to conceal the original income, nor did fail to document both the income and outlay. On one level, the filed charges are complaints about the accounting headings under which the items were recorded. In one case, the fact that employee benefits that were neither salary nor scheduled bonuses were classified separately.

Another complaint revolves around tuition payments – what amounts to company scholarships for qualified employees.

If scholarships are personal income – they are subject to payroll taxes. However, that would mean ALL scholarships are taxable income and it would be illegal for the District Attorney to apply their charges law only to the Trump Organization.

In accordance with the New York City case, it is clear that any scholarship – including those granted by universities to the benefit of their employees – must be reported as income. If you "earned" a scholarship, you worked for it and earned it – it is earned taxable income. Arguing otherwise will tie up the courts for decades, or demonstrate the legal incompetence of both the New York District Attorney and Attorney General.

But that's just the opinion of a non-lawyer.

The scholarships are just one article of the first charge of 15 that were accepted by the New York County Grand Jury.

In some charges, they question where the accused lived for the purpose of a resident tax filing – of note is the inability of the accusers to specify which jurisdiction was offended. They say "state or any political subdivision of the state."

But, if the act was not specific to New York County, how did a borough of Manhattan District Attorney gain jurisdiction for the filing?

Moreover, given the number of tax record audits we can expect to have been done at various levels, what the NYCDA is asserting is the gross incompetence of both Federal and State tax auditors. Maybe Vance and James are also preparing a case against the respective auditors for conspiracy — conspiring with the Trump Organization to defraud the government.

It all hangs on whether the costs were booked properly – something we could reasonably expect a routine government audit should have determined.

The final charge is one of the erasure *"with the intent to defraud,"* of a *"true entry"* appearing in *"Donald J. Trump's*

Detailed General Ledger." The implication is that it was a tax or income-related entry posted in the appropriate ledger.

The charge states an erasure of a line item amounted to Falsifying Business Records – this could mean that making any corrections to a ledger is a criminal act. However, the charge is bogus and a waste of taxpayer money, if the entry in question appears in any other corporate ledger or was deemed not to be a corporate income or expense item.

What we see upon reading the charges is the classic act of a dishonest prosecutor utilizing overly generalized legalistic phrasing. The jurisdiction where the defendant should be the legal residence is the where they registered to vote and where any of their motor vehicles were registered and insured.

However, once again we see something with significant ramifications for anyone whose work requires them to be away from their home. It would be interesting, using NYCDA logic, to discover if American Soldiers stationed overseas are legally obligated to pay income taxes to the nation in which they reside while working. If American law supports the NYCDA, then the foreign nations have a right to invoke it to collect taxes from the US military.

Again, not a lawyer. Just a citizen wondering where the NYCDA gets the right to attempt the alteration of American law for personal benefit or to further New York's political animosity toward Trump.

This work is being published in July 2021; with time the game will play out enough for readers to determine reality. But the pattern of attacks since 2016 indicates the process of attacks will soon involve charges against the only Orthodox Jew in the Trump family.

Those attacking Trump consistently manipulate race and bigotry as the core of their actions. Early on they these bigots masquerading as Democrats probed various attack strategies, but outright anti-Semitism toward Ivanka and her husband was an issue they had to mute because of their need to keep both the California and New York Congressman and Senators on board.

We can expect a series of nonsense charges will be filed against Ivanka. Unless they become desperate, openly attack her husband would expose their true destructive agenda.

Readers need not wait to confirm that animosity sells – this historically known fact was confirmed in a modern context and documented in a National Academy of Sciences paper – *"Out-group animosity drives engagement on social media"* – that was published on 29 June 2021.

Up until now, I have referred to them as *"The Other,"* but the term *"Out-group"* has potential. It certainly describes those who have backed Trump, and that reality explains the insane obsession with Trump's tax returns.

For a District Attorney, there is enormous personal gain by going after the "Rich White Guy" in a city where Black-on-Black crime defines many prosecutions. This is especially true when the political environment ignores reality and considers all Black defendants to be the result of racism.

They do not want people to know or understand that, in terms of race, Blacks are responsible for more murders than any other ethnic group – 52.5% of all murders – predominantly representing Blacks killing Blacks. Only about 12% of killings are interracial.

As bad as it might seem, New York State ranks ninth in the nation, For murders, California is your place – number one in the nation. After that, it's Texas and Florida.

All four states have a going Hispanic population which will get much larger under the Biden Open Border policies. Statisticians are reporting a growing number of Hispanic gangs and their link to increased criminal activity. But that activity is consistent with calls to defund the police in communities where illegal immigrants are settling.

As Democratic Representative Alexandria Ocasio-Cortez

said, "*Defunding police means defunding police. It does not mean budget tricks or funny math.*" AOC's Missouri colleague Cori Bush supported the objective – "*So yes, defund your butts. Defund you.*" And New York Mayor Bill De Blasio acted on the demand by removing a Billion dollars from the NYPD budget.

Defunding the police is, apparently, an act of supporting racial equality. There are no equivalent moves to improve the funding for education and resources in minority communities. Why should there be? After all, scholarship is number one on the list for Confucius, Marx, and Biblical mercantile commerce.

The issue of racism was redefined under an academic-sounding title – Critical race theory {CRT} – which strives to redefine history as institutionalized racism that has nothing to do with biological fact or the reality of evolution.

The issue is a denial of the fact that races evolved based on environmental conditions and all animals are programmed to react negatively toward members of the "*Out-group.*"

If we were not programmed as we are, beneficial genetic mutations would not replicate in the manner they do. Another way to view it, humanity would never have evolved into either Neanderthal or Homo Sapiens – it is doubtful we would even have achieved the ape-related stage.

Again we can look to the Bible and see that the Shepherd Kings who devised it understood the reality. The marriage laws are breeding patterns whose basic construct emerges from the segregation of each tribal group, with a set of rules that would allow those who were "superior' to move up the mating tree.

It is a basic rule of nature that has leaders mate with – or marry and procreate with – members of their own strata. That same rule of nature allows those with superior traits to advance into the upper echelon. This is true within a given racial group and across groups.

An Indian-Brahmin sex-based joke: "*Once you've gone brown, all the others let you down.*" It's inter-racial, racist, and declares Indian Aryan superiority.

India's caste system similar to the tribal out outlined in the Old Testament – it was distorted by the British. But that's a different version of the *"Out-group"* issue.

An *"Out-group"* issue that concerns us can be seen in the algorithm utilized by FaceBook.

In 2018, a Facebook research team made the company aware of the fact their *"algorithms exploit the human brain's attraction to divisiveness."* In effect, telling the company that it was profiting from the promotion of *"Out-group"* attacks.

This is not a surprise. It is quite intentional. The news media or public forum attracts the most attention and gains the broadest readership through the "If it bleeds, it leads" form of editing. This means they always place a negative spin on things and avoid balancing the facts.

An example is routinely found in articles that mention Trump not having served in the military and, while classified 1-A received educational exemptions; they mention his *"bone spurs"* – but neglect to say they were confirmed by x-rays. They ignore the fact that, at the time of the medical diagnosis, Trump had reached exemption age and the draft was being brought to an end. The *"bone spurs"* were meaningless.

Omitted from the articles is the fact that Joe Biden never served, and his basis for avoiding the draft was identified in a popular song of the era, *"Draft Dodger Rag."* {?Plagiarism?}

Unlike Trump, Biden's documented history of honesty includes lies about his past and Law School plagiarism, which when exposed during one of his campaigns, was cited as the reason he withdrew from that attempt to become a Presidential nominee.

When we look at his books, they offer no vision. Rather, they present tear-jerking hardships involving the loss of family members. My attitude toward this might seem cold to those who have never been there. But, thanks to *"Toxic Shock"* – the tampon-related staff infection of the late 1960s, at the age of 23, I became a widower with an infant son.

Plagiarizing Trump, since taking office Biden has shown he wants to see the positive. Trump saw good people among the bad and like I have done here, seen in Hitler's writings things that are positives or offer lessons in acquiring leadership.

In June 2021, Biden tongue-lashed a reporter over a question and then said he's looking for uplifting questions. He did not want to fall prey to the take of media tactic which would make him subject to the same type of attacker that welcomed Trump's election.

Biden has a firewall – media attacks on Trump provide the reaction the media thrives on. This is exactly why there is a FaceBook algorithm that ensures the survival of *"Out-Group"* bigotry and lies.

As the research established, negative attacks will *"raise a perceptual screen through which the individual tends to see what is favorable to [their] partisan orientation."* However, as with Prohibition, what is achieved is the opposite of the desired effect.

In that light, we see the attacks on *Roe v Wade* and the move to return abortions being illegal. People wave the Bible and talk about the sanctity of life while ignoring the fact the Bible mandates taking a herbal remedy that would mystically induce an abortion if the fetus is not their husband's. If there is no husband, it would appear abortion is mandatory.

As we know, *Right-to-Life* group members have opposed medical care for all – most importantly, they do not advocate for the medical care that would ensure the health and wellbeing of the fetus through gestation and into the first two years of life.

The reality is, they will allow both mother and fetus to die, rather than save the life of the mother – because they do not care about life. All they want is to ensure a child that will die anyway, or effectively live life as a non-productive vegetable, will be forced upon the parents.

The *Right-to-Life* goal is harming as many as possible.

Were it otherwise they would oppose the type of mass destruction and war initiating military spending demonstrated by America over the past 70-years.

Misrepresentation of true goal – the *Right-to-Life* lie – is an example generally accompanied by an omission of facts. The facts about *Roe v Wade* being that a year after the ruling, abortions dropped and the number of children – in and out of marriage – increased.

The number of unwed mothers increased after women were given the time and freedom to think about their desire to have a child. Prior to *Roe v Wade*, the focus was on finding an abortionist. But knowing that they could simply visit a clinic allowed them to consider the possibilities associated with being a parent.

If the *Right-to-Life* goal was really about the sanctity of life, rather than harming people, they would advocate for free medical care, a Universal Basic Income, and – at a minimum – a fifty percent cut in the Federal military budget.

Historical evidence clearly establishes that most attacks targeting personal choice or lifestyle decisions will achieve the opposite of the stated allegedly desired goal.

Leaders understand this. Those whose leadership goal is personal power and harm to the masses, utilize it. As a rule, a third of the population will follow blindly behind those who seem to be leaders and are advocating in language consistent with some "traditional belief."

Those seeking to take leadership positions are aware of this normal animalistic response and use it to manipulate those of lesser mentality – *the Emperor's New Clothes*, asserted that only the wisest could see them, thus the idiots pretended to be wise. The Emperor stood naked before them and they were in argumentative denial of the reality.

Gee, blame "*Whitey*" for your problems and show your anger by burning down your own neighborhood. Pelosi can stand at a podium and insight the masses to rebel or engage in violence; when the wrong masses take her advice, she and her associates, who advocated violence, denounce Trump because he told his rally to PEACEFULLY march over to Congress and express their views. The speeches on both sides are a matter of video news records.

True Leaders are wise, they see the truth that is before them. If you're an idiot if you don't see the factious clothes, because the con-artist said only the wisest can, silence the wise.

Where do "Out-Groups" come from?

In terms of evolution, among sentient creatures, they are those who see things differently. Some latch on to tradition with no change, others are always looking for change or a way to rephrase and restructure the old to fit the current environment.

This is how evolution works. *Creationists* hold that all things were created as a constant, there is no real evolutionary change that deviates significantly from the original design.

In terms of racism or antisemitism, evolution shows that normal breeding habits turn an ethnic group within a species into a race, subspecies, or different completely different entity.

Races evolved to adapt to environmental conditions. If the evolutionary change is beneficial, it will spread throughout the species. However, during the process, and to achieve what that evolutionary trait testing period demands – those who are different become the focus of distrust.

It doesn't matter which group you are a part of – original or mutated – the other group is the "Out-Group."

Evolution is a process by which there are both visible and invisible effects to separate the groups and drive one toward extinction – think Neanderthal vs Homo Sapiens.

While we know the Neanderthal went extinct, there was

still an element in them that were attractive to Homo Sapiens and those appear in the remnants of Neanderthal DNA that is now being discovered as part of the modern human population.

When intellectual evolution occurs, we see technological advances in one group which are copied by the others. These advances are not necessarily the result of higher IQ, but rather are a manifestation of a genetic abnormality involving curiosity and a form of dyslexia – seeing things differently and, in that context, processing data differently.

There is NO Master Race.

But the idea was used by Hitler and others for as long as there has been recorded history. When some group claims to be *"Children of God"* they are in reality asserting they are the Master Race. In the Bible, one of the primary aspects of the story of Noah is that the flood kills all those who are *"Men of Renown"* whose fathers were the sons of the deity. The old Master Race is killed by a deliberate act of the deity whose sons spawned them.

That is one means of creating leadership – eliminate any who a position of power based on them being, genetically, the Master Race. By applying the term to the Aryans, Hitler utilized the traditional approach and defined the Hebrews as the "Men of Renown" who were to be removed. When he was denied the ability to remove, he or someone in the Nazis organization came up with *"the Final Solution"* to *"the Jewish Question."*

But even there, when speaking of *"the Jewish Question,"* the Nazis were addressing something with a long history.

In an article published in February 1844, Bruno Bauer explored the idea: *"The German Jews desire emancipation. What kind of emancipation do they desire? Civic, political emancipation."*

Substitute Negro or Black for Jews and the assertion is moved into 20th-century America and carried into the current post-first-black-president rhetoric. At the same time, it reflects the condition of American slaves under both the White and free Black masters.

Bauer goes on to respond that no Germans are free:

"No one in Germany is politically emancipated. We ourselves are not free. How are we to free you? You Jews are egoists if you demand a special emancipation for yourselves as Jews. As Germans, you ought to work for the political emancipation of Germany, and as human beings, for the emancipation of mankind, and you should feel the particular kind of your oppression and your shame not as an exception to the rule, but on the contrary as a confirmation of the rule."

And then he continues with a response that can easily be applied to modern America and the lack of resources devoted to the general welfare:

"Or do the Jews demand the same status as Christian subjects of the state? In that case, they recognize that the Christian state is justified and they recognize, too, the regime of general oppression. Why should they disapprove of their special yoke if they approve of the general yoke? Why should the German be interested in the liberation of the Jew, if the Jew is not interested in the liberation of the German?

The Christian state knows only privileges."

Today the call is *"White Privilege."* The would-be harm doers are using the same techniques and same logic that existed nearly two centuries ago.

Obviously, quoting Bauer's 1844 Deutsch-Französische Jahrbücher article would only emphasize how repetitive history is. We would learn that there were Jewish rights similar to the race-based priorities enjoyed by blacks – places in universities set aside for "racial balance" and ignoring standardized testing.

We have the words of President Biden that he chose his

running mate based on gender and race – without any regard for the objective qualifications to be if needed, his replacement.

Harris is proud of a prosecutorial record Representative Tulsi Gabbard (D-Hawaii) warranted an apology: *"The people who suffered under your reign as prosecutor, you owe them an apology."*

Gabbard pointed out that Harris knowingly blocked the evidence of innocence so that she could keep the innocent man on death row – a black man convicted of a crime the only eye-witness said was committed by three blond-haired white men. But Harris claims blackness and that makes it OK.

As Deepak Chopra said: *"Every time you are tempted to react in the same old way, ask if you want to be a prisoner of the past or a pioneer of the future. The past is closed and limited; the future is open and free."*

The idea that *"the past is closed"* is something popular fiction rejects. In 1895, H. G. Wells expressed that rejection in the science fiction novella, *The Time Machine.*

In that pre-turn-of-the-century era, time travel became a popular genre. Apparently, the foundation laid out in an 1881 story, *"The Clock that Went Backward."*

In science, physicists were beginning to view time as a fourth dimension and 25-years later Eienstein would produce his Theory of General relativity.

Since then, writers of fiction have loved to play with the topic. We can go *"Back to the Future"* or engage in activities that alter timelines and change history – which brings us to the reason for this topical divergence.

People rant about Hitler and the Nazis, they play with the idea of going back in history to kill Hitler; they believe that would stop the Japanese fighting China, or affect the Holocaust.

The people who play with such ideas are not leaders.

As Garden of Eden Serpent, they ignore the ramifications of the various actions. More important, they seek to alter the storm while ignoring the Butterfly flapping its wings.

It's a game of chess. What was the greatest cause of the Second World War?

Wasn't it the First World War – a war that started with a madman assassinating Archduke Franz Ferdinand of Austria?

Wasn't that war and his experience as a wounded soldier what motivated Hitler? Wasn't it the animosity between Britain and Germany that defined the punishing terms of the Treaty of Versailles and established the political propaganda groundwork that gave rise to social disruption that Hitler was protesting?

The horrors of the holocaust would not have happened, if not for Gavrilo Princip, a 19-year-old revolutionary, seeking what? A monument, not unlike the one for George Floyd, says: "*From this place, on 28 June 1914, Gavrilo Princip, expressed with his shot the people's revolt against tyranny and their centuries-old struggle for freedom.*"

The killing of a husband and wife, petty nobility, became the immediate cause of death for 20 million people – half of whom were civilians. Then the ripple effect caused an artist to become an author and then German Führer, causing the death of 75 million people – 20 million military, 40 million civilians, plus six million genocidal murders.

The butterfly actions of a 19-year-old "leader" gave rise to a chain of events that killed the equivalent of the 1914 United States population; it brought about the creation of the Atomic Bomb. And finally, one boy's actions created the environment that brought about the Russian Revolution, the Cold War, the Korean War, and the Vietnam War.

We focus on *Hitler* and totally forget about *Princip*.

It would be nice if, just for once, science fiction writers would focus on the historic butterfly.

Is there a butterfly currently forming from its chrysalis?

If so? Is it to be found in the Out-Group, or among those who are supposedly our leaders.

CHAPTER Fourteen - LEADERSHIP

Who is a Leader?

What is Leadership?

You made it this far, so you have an image buried in the back of your mind – bring it forward.

You got this far. You're a leader. The only issue is where you are on the leadership spectrum.

Most leaders keep a low profile. As we know, a hammer strikes the nail whose head is raised. We attack those who, like Trump, show their ambition through a desire to be recognized and remembered. We also attack those devoid of ambition, or who seek to avoid recognition for their noble deeds.

False leaders demand people "work" and then give them meaningless tasks.

These leaders will tell someone to carry a bucket of sand from point A to point B; then carry the same filled bucket from point B back to point A – they call it workfare or non-essential employment. The purpose is to prevent individuals from doing those things that achieve something meaningful – like caring for their child, cleaning their house, or going on interviews that have the potential for gainful employment.

Since, by definition, an individual on public assistance lacks sufficient resources to meet their basic survival needs – they have no money and public assistance must be increased to cover the costs of transportation to the workfare location.

False leaders use moralistic arguments to inflict harm on the general society. They follow a doctrine that can be given the litmus test of *"The Most Harm to the Most People."*

False leaders will ask how we can afford Universal Basic Income. Since it does away with the most of public assistance, unemployment checks, and the Income Tax personal deduction, it should save money while increasing GDP and tax revenues.

Since the wealthy enjoy the same personal deductions as the poor, giving them the same UBI doesn't matter. And as we know from Scandinavian countries, having higher tax rates can be meaningless when basic costs are covered by the state.

There is a false metric that focuses on tax rates rather than net disposable income after both taxes and common costs are accounted for. But basic accounting goes against the reality of those who want to harm society while enjoying personal gain.

False leaders believe in *"Open Borders."*

They know the result is to attract individuals who cannot speak or read the language. Since they have no employment lined up, they become public charges. And when their numbers are largely composed of children in need of education, they are a burden on the communities in which they settle.

For the false leader, these individuals are warm bodies that can be used to gerrymander representative seats and bring in State and Federal funds to benefit their voter base. In turn, that base donates money to their campaign funds – money that can later be syphoned off by the leader or their associates.

Ultimately, the general population and economy are the victims and pay the price.

True leaders develop and promote concepts that better society. If they wish to bring in Climate Change refugees, they first establish systems for integrating the individuals into the culture. This could include placing them in communities whose resources are underutilized.

One aspect of integration is an avoidance of any form of ghetto or urban *"endogamic"* community structure. Ideally, the new arrivals would be placed in rural settings in low population states.

A certain degree of *"endogamic"* community structure cannot be avoided, but if the citizen and newcomer population are evenly balanced, social integration becomes easier.

Absent an urban conflict setting, each group will teach

the other and rural resources will be better utilized. This would also strengthen rural leadership development.

A leader can be an individual with no followers. Yet they can engage in acts that shape history.

We saw this in 2001 when nineteen individuals engaged in a suicidal attack on the New York World Trade Center and their action served to initiate a nineteen-year retaliatory "War on Terrorism" – resulting in the death of an uncounted number of Muslims.

Another example is the 1914 act of murder by *Gavrilo Princip* resulted in two World wars, the death of 100 million, and, arguably, the 1918 influenza pandemic – whose spread was facilitated by soldiers returning from the First World War.

Sometimes, being a leader is just being the one who kicks over the first domino. It's the butterfly that flaps its wings at just the right time to create a *"perfect storm"* that brings about *"The Most Harm to the Most People."*

Ideally, a leader is a person who acts with peaceful intent and a clearly defined positive goal.

Being a leader is having a skill set that others might envy – being a hunter who bags a surplus of game. The hunter hunts when conditions are right, they do not wait to be out of food.

Generating a surplus is the basis for learning to preserve and store your food. A surplus can be anything that's "extra" – in a cash economy it was your change; you always spend paper, and when you get change, you drop it in a piggy bank or jar. It's amazing how much you will accumulate for that "rainy day."

Observed behavior creates a surplus of knowledge about the work of others. It is also the basis for all learning.

When I was a child I observed, when I was a bit older, I came to understand that there is a process for learning – *"Look, Listen, Copy, Practice until you get it right; then be creative."*

Those who reach a stage of creativity and invention are leaders – they need not have followers, if what they do has value to the herd or tribe, followers will emerge.

Even if those followers never seem to emerge, if you are doing what you enjoy, it will give you satisfaction.

Enjoyment is accompanied by a pleasant form of hard work and determination – and those two things are associated with ambition. Unlike many things associated with ambition, that which you enjoy imposes little or no stress. You rule your body and mind; you learn more, are more, and do more than those who are always stressed.

As they say: *"Time flies when you are having fun."* So set aside time for those you love, or make them an integral part of what you are doing.

"Look, Listen, Copy, Practice until you get it right; then be creative."

Societal fools fail to grasp reality – creativity and wisdom begin with plagiarism.

All wise people copy what came before and worked.

The intelligent, the creative, the leaders, go a step beyond and see where things have changed or can be improved upon. These are the leaders. And when they prove correct they are the leaders worthy of being followed.

Some behave as leaders but only destroy.

Galileo Galilei observed that: *"You cannot teach a man anything; you can only help him discover it in himself."*

If you observe that which is around you and then look inside, you will discover who you are by seeing who is like you.

Those who serve as Leaders can take pride in being on a journey of self-discovery. Upon seeing a path worthy of walking they invite us all to follow along. They do not insist, or coerce, or infringe upon the path we want to follow. If our path does not corrupt theirs, they wish us a happy journey and proceed down the road they have chosen. Only the deceivers of men will insist that their path is the only one.

Take a lesson from history. Things are proposed and die. Then, if they are rational things, they are reborn. Ideas that are proposed by one generation might be ahead of their time.

It is a wondrous thing to look back and discover you are seeing the future.

The ancient Greeks and Egyptians had simple batteries they used to electroplate jewelry; they had hydraulic systems to "magically" open or close doors; they built enormous structures without the cranes or massive machines.

However, people would rather believe that space-aliens are responsible for ancient technological wonders – their ancestors couldn't be intelligent and accomplished.

In 1984, Erich Von Daniken's best-selling "Chariots of the Gods" established just how acceptable it is for the general public to diminish ancestral human accomplishments.

Von Daniken tapped into the negative aspect of society.

Humans lack the confidence to accept their own abilities; they would prefer to see non-existent clothes and believe their ability to see what is not there proves their wisdom.

The fun part is that people do not see what is there. They fail to see the *"elephant in the room,"* or notice when something is wrong.

Maybe you looked at the cover of this book and noticed something was wrong. I'm not talking about the shape of the board, or even the fact three key pieces are of different colors and styles.

Those who know the game of chess might have noticed the strategic "Easter Egg" error; it's hidden in the imagery as an error in the tactical pattern.

When the other guy's rules are rigged against you – when they create a no-win scenario – like Captain Kirk addressing the Kobayashi Maru scenario, you change the rules.

Relative to the opponent, the position was altered in two

ways. One is the obvious lack of a place for them to put their pieces. But, did you see the other deviation? When you do, think about how it would change the game.

For now, let's turn our attention to the *"Big Lie"* and how accusing one side of it conceals that the accuser is the liar.

Trump *"Lost the 2020 Election."* But that does not alter the fact some irregularities need to be addressed; it is also a fact that a lot of the metrics argue a victory for Trump. We must also acknowledge that four states account for about a third of the national population.

Of 331.5 million people, the states of California (39.6m), Texas (29.7m), Florida (21.9), and New York (19.3m) account for 110.5 million. These same four states benefit from the influx of individuals from south of the border.

Every million individuals who cross the border illegally will increase the population of these four states by about one percent. That number was exceeded in the first seven months of 2021. The fact that Pelosi and Schumer are avoiding that reality is the true *"Big Lie"* intended to harm the nation.

Unfortunately, there are con artists who seek to deceive and invite us to see that which is not there – they proclaim the wondrous beauty of the *Emperor's New Clothes*, and the vision they know the fools will accept.

The fools live in the realm of ignorance.

Education is a path to enlightenment. It is learning from that which has gone before. It is plagiarism of experience and acquired knowledge derived from error or success.

Education deals with the world and its rules.

But, when we speak of enlightenment we are speaking of the intangible world of emotion and caring. A positive leader has their feet planted securely in both worlds.

To be enlightened we must care about everyone else. We must care about our environment, our home, that place we are sharing with all other people on this planet. And we must be selfish enough to put a long-term benefit before some short-term act of "*political correctness*" or transitory personal gain.

As Jane Goodall expressed a variation on the concept of "*Wisdom, Knowledge, and Understanding,*" or caring, "*Only if we understand can we care. Only if we care will we help. Only if we help shall they be saved.*"

An interesting aspect of the pronoun "they" is the one you are saving is "you".

You are the leader.

You are the one who teaches your child, your niece or nephew, your neighbor's child, through your words and deeds.

Do you care?

Justin Bieber had a song that began with the words "*I'm at a party I don't wanna be at / And I don't ever wear a suit and tie, yeah / Wondering if I could sneak out the back / Nobody's even looking me in my eyes / Then you take my hand / ...*"

Then it addresses its title "*I Don't Care.*"

First Lady Melania Trump wore a coat upon which were the words, "*I Don't Care.*"

Curiously, the song is about caring. It's about just how meaningless things become when you are with someone with whom you feel an emotional connection. "'*Cause I don't care as long as you just hold me near ...*"

Caring is what life is about, it's what leadership should be about. If you are a leader, you care. You exercise that care with the one you are with, at your place of employment, and in those, you elect as your representatives.

But, interestingly, not caring can be an expression of caring.

Every individual has the potential to be a leader. Most prefer to be part of the Herd. That does not diminish the reality that they are leadership material, it only means their time has not come. Though it does come when they vote, or when they become parents.

It comes when they decide on the necessity to vaccinate – will they endanger themselves and others?

As stated, Covid-19 is a culling virus, it's "harmless," it's a virus that only harms those who have other life-ending issues.

But their "*I Don't Care*" mindset exposes their desire to inflict "*The Most Harm to the Most People*" – at heart, they are no different than any other suicidal terrorist.

It took only five days, 17 July to 22 July, for Monkeypox to go from two cases to a possible 200 cases. How much faster could it spread? How would it like to be joined with a culling virus?

Before a vaccination can protect the body, the disease or virus must first infect it. It's similar to saying a lock prevents opening only if someone wants to open what the lock is keeping closed. If you don't care about the contents, you don't need the lock. Anti-vaxxers don't care if they live or die.

During the period when the immune system is killing the invading illness, the illness can be transmitted and, if the test is timed properly, vaccinated individuals could test positive. But there is no doubt that the virus would prefer not to be impeded by a vaccine.

The risk to the unvaccinated increases as we restrict the number of bodies that can provide it a home. Vaccination can be viewed as creating a segregated neighborhood where a given "species" is not allowed but might occasionally visit.

Covid-19 is a culling virus; those who chose to remain unvaccinated are either declaring they are perfectly healthy, or wish to assist in the culling and don't mind becoming a victim.

It's an exercise in freewill; so long as it doesn't harm others, rejecting vaccines should be allowed. However, anti-vaxxers are a prophesied "*end of times*" variation on *Gavrilo Princip* – knowing this, is there a way to counteract them?

Where is the leadership that will find a means to stop the killing virus – the Monkeypox or any of the dozens of ancient virus variations emerging from melting glaciers?

We need the prophesied leader, a man who can unite the world and, as Trekkies would say, create an Earth Federation.

There are three types of people in the world. The largest group are simply members of the herd. They graze and follow along with the majority.

Next, we have leaders – people who have a purpose and a defined goal. This group can be subdivided into visible and invisible leaders.

Every day, the invisible leaders work toward goals that are as simple as being happy. Often they are amazed at how quickly time passes. They know the various emotions but are not controlled by them. Positive emotions do exert a strong influence on their daily lives.

We all know visible leaders. They are driven by the need to be seen and are often associated with leadership that enjoys basking in their limelight but has no interest in being the target of naysayers.

Decide who you are and act accordingly.

Within a herd, some individuals are catalysts for history. They have no defined objective, no political purpose behind their actions; yet through actions, history will be transformed for better or worse. Because, like the *"Butterfly Effect,"* they are generally unnoticed and unknown finding an example becomes difficult.

Then we have the catalytic leader – an individual who, in one context, might go unnoticed or become a footnote in some category.

On 30 March 1981, John W. Hinckley Jr. attempted the assassination of President Ronald Reagan – that added him to the roster of assassins whose names are generally forgotten.

Hinckley catalyzed nothing.

A little under four months earlier, on 8 December 1980, Mark David Chapman assassinated the former *Beatles* musician and songwriter John Lennon.

As with Hinckley, Chapman was a catalyst for nothing.

However, when *Gavrilo Princip* committed murder, he had a political agenda and that made him a catalytic leader – a person who political or social objective who triggered events he could never have foreseen.

When, on 11 September 2001 (911), Al-Qaeda operatives destroyed the World Trade Center, they did so at the direction of Osama bin Laden – a radical leader whose own videotaped words revealed his surprise at the building collapsing.

As we know, bin Laden was from a family with close ties to the Saudi royal family; the modern Kingdom of Saudi Arabia has, through various incarnations, been a dynastic Arab factor in history since the founding of Islam. The Saudis achieved attack on the World Trade Center of the catalytic-leadership role it will have when the inter-factional conflict within Islam finally starts World War Three and is resolved after fourteen-hundred years of gestation.

For now, Middle East nations form a wealthy oil-based economy. Their wealth has given them military independence and the means to acquire modern weapons of mass destruction.

Just as advanced industrialized nations adapt to Climate Change by turning to renewable-based electricity, the emerging nations have been acquiring renewable energy resources as the basis for development. After 2025, the need for oil and other carbon fuels should return to pre-industrial demand levels – the basis for Middle Eastern wealth will evaporate.

Before that happens – it will take several generations for oil to becomes as meaningless as cordwood – declining use of oil will catalyze a *"final solution"* Islamic War. It was predicted in their scripture, and all that is required is a charismatic leader to serve as their "Messiah."

Ultimately, the new age will see the creation of a dozen, or baker's dozen, cultural ethnic groups. As seen in the Biblical marriage laws codification of endogamy, self-segregation is a natural state which allowed the formation of a nation where the differences could be filtered out over time.

Various racial groups might complain about segregation, but they are the ones initiating it. Through their endogamous practices, they work against integration. It doesn't matter if it is based on skin tone, religious mysticism, or anything else they chose to make them different – the ultimate result is still self-segregation and self-exclusion from the overall culture.

By demonstrating a selective view on integration, they ensure integration will not work. In a biblical context, the idea of segregation as a response to out-groups is deemed wrong and we are told the foreigner should be treated as a native – even as the natives divided themselves into tribes. The Biblical tribal structure was an endogamous culture with well-defined borders that could only be cross by those with an education.

Because endogamy is natural, the laws created a rational basis for the process in the form of thirteen tribal groups – the twelve tribes plus a thirteenth composed of the highly educated and high earners who instinctively gravitate away from their endogamic culture.

As we have seen in recent years, American culture seems to oppose and dislike the educated, while also relying on them to keep the economy going.

In the Biblical context, the self-segregated reach a point where they acquire sufficient knowledge to marry outside of the native tribal group – defined as "Exogamy" – graduating into the leadership.

If America were a true "melting pot" culture, the guiding rule would be to practice exogamy. We would neutralize most forms of religion and welcome a broader practice of interracial marriage. We would celebrate our history – not try to cancel it so it can be repeated. We would celebrate the fact we overcame the negatives and moved forward.

Those whose ancestral history includes slaves should be grateful. If not for their slave ancestors, and the white masters who mated with them, they would not exist. The racist "one-drop rule" reflects the degree of interbreeding that defines the history of slavery. Comically, with the advent of DNA ancestral tracing, many whose families histories include white racists can now be pointed to as "black."

As we know from Barack Obama, who is a tenth cousin to George Washington, and a descendant of the 4-Sisters, being half-African is not an issue. Regardless of an individual's apparent racial affiliation, education and the degree to which you practice endogamy is the only meaningful issue.

The stronger your ties to endogamy, the more harmful you are as a leader. Currently, harmful leaders are in control.

With time, all cultures create a means of addressing the out-group aspect of endogamy. On one level they conform to the biblical Levite or European nobility. On another, they are weaponized in the way Marx and the current manifestation of American liberals have done with their focus on the 1-percent.

Is it a persistent use of rhetorical lies, misrepresentation of facts, to achieve a transient benefit for oneself?

That seems to be the historical case. And the historical technique is to utilize the inability of a segment of the masses to see reality.

When Bauer was addressing *"the Jewish Question"*, he was looking at the idea that the Jew wanted *"equal treatment"* within a society where most people were oppressed. He saw the Jew as someone whose frame of reference assumed they were Levites – part of the leadership class – and, therefore, did not identify with the common masses.

Bauer was seeing people who, he claimed, did not see the reality of what was happening to others in society – people too focused on their state of being to show empathy for their non-Jewish neighbors.

However, Bruno Bauer was writing in 1844 and did not recognize the importance of a group mindset. If we look around today, we see a global population of less than fifty million has a place that is securely situated among the leadership. But even in decades leading to his era, it was people like Haym Salomon, a Polish-born Jewish businessman, who would step forward to finance the American Revolution.

Jews have always been a catalyst for change.

The average German that Bauer used as his model did not see themself as a leader – they saw themselves as slaves, serfs, peasants, eating pork, drinking beer, and fighting the wars of others as mercenaries whose pay went to their feudal lords. That German self-image was what Friedrich Engels and Karl Marx were addressing.

In 1844, Bauer was consciously ignoring the fact that it was Marx, a Jew, who was calling the superior treatment of the masses – rather than the *"equal treatment"* Bauer was focused on denouncing.

In modern America, the black community likes minority status; they hold tight to it while other minorities move forward and prosper. The same can be said for Palestine Muslims, who would rather spend their money promoting hate and harm to their neighbor, rather than use the same money to advance and prosper.

In America, that mentality has created a nation that is devoted to foreign "military interventions" – spending more on destructive military tools than the next ten highest-spending nations. The quality of American civilian leadership is such that, even with the huge budget, America could not win the Korean War, could not win in Vietnam, and, for twenty years, devoted its money to a conflict that has only strengthened and unified the opposition – preparing them for World War Three.

It's comical. Hate ensures the evolutionary division.

When the shepherd kings produced the Old Testament, they stated that their laws and practices would dominate global practices. They did not teach hate. And today we see that 3% of the population occupies 30% of top positions, and the share is larger if we consider the POTUS Cousins.

Our Leaders would be wise to heed the words of self-help writer Guy Finley: *"What we find in life is based on where we put our attention. When we focus on the small worlds our thoughts create, we miss out on the beauty and possibilities we are meant to enjoy."* And when our leaders push our focus into *"small worlds,"* the possibilities that lay within our grasp are stolen away.

The Cancel Culture enjoys looking back and attempting to change the history that made today possible. But they should be looking forward, and taking a first step toward the creation of the next and better place.

To see the world differently, to create that new world, we must change our belief system. We must dismiss references to that which was harmful – stop living there, and let it go – now is what has meaning, and, tomorrow comes, even when you are focused on yesterday. But, by focusing on yesterday, you have wasted all the opportunities that are available today.

Granted, there are times when looking back is the proper thing to do. In the days before the "Tall Ships," the galley was propelled by rowers whose power came from facing backward toward a leader who looks forward.

It's OK to look back if it is to watch a leader with a clear vision of what is ahead. Leaders can lead from the rear.

Leaders think, they find the good among the bad. Those who do not think are not leaders, they are destroyers who can only see things as being bad. They cannot grasp the reality of *"Good people on both sides."* They only see bad people, and then, only among those, they seek to destroy.

As I showed with the imposition of Revelation prophecy onto the Holocaust, an extreme negative can be a positive. This is important when, like my family, at least a thousand family members were killed by the Nazis.

The Nazis were evil. But, if you read Hitler, you see he advocated deporting Jews to other countries – and when that failed, a *"Final Solution"* was proposed by members of the Nazi leadership. The Nazis did not invent the *"Final Solution"* – it was standard practice among Catholics and Protestants. It was the Inquisition and the distribution of those smallpox-infected blankets to Native Americans.

It is known that *the Madagascar Plan* was devised by Adolf Eichmann – it would have deported Jews to the French Colony if the plan had not been obstructed by a British naval blockade. For about 300-years, the British had demonstrated their anti-Semitism by closing their kingdom to Jews.

Many of the worst military outcomes suffered by the British in both World Wars are attributed to their military anti-Semites rejecting orders from Jewish Generals.

As mentioned in *Jonathon's POTUS Cousins*, historians now speculate that the Battle of Dunkirk would have favored Britain and the mass evacuation would never have happened, if the British had listened to and obeyed the directions of their Jewish Commanding General.

There are good leaders and horrible ones. The good see good and work for positive outcomes. The others see only the bad; they lie and proclaim "overwhelming evidence" of the bad – but when called upon to reveal it, produce nothing.

History reveals the importance of the 4-Sisters. It tells us about the qualities that make good leaders; it reveals there are repetitive patterns of events; it brings forth people whose function is to detract us from the catalysts –the serpent in the garden.

In 2024, the United States gets a chance to play Adam.

www.ingramcontent.com/pod-product-compliance
Lightning Source LLC
Chambersburg PA
CBHW061338250726
48657CB00004B/1221